CORBIÈRE, MALLARMÉ, VALÉRY

PRESERVATIONS AND COMMENTARY

STANFORD
FRENCH AND ITALIAN
STUDIES

volume XXIII

ANMA LIBRI

CORBIÈRE, MALLARMÉ, VALÉRY

PRESERVATIONS AND COMMENTARY

ROBERT L. MITCHELL

1981
ANMA LIBRI

Stanford French and Italian Studies is a collection of scholarly publications devoted to the study of French and Italian literature and language, culture and civilization. Occasionally it will allow itself excursions into related Romance areas.

Stanford French and Italian Studies will publish books, monographs, and collections of articles centering around a common theme, and is open also to scholars associated with academic institutions other than Stanford.

The collection is published for the Department of French and Italian, Stanford University by Anma Libri.

ACKNOWLEDGMENTS

Portions of the Corbière translations presented herein (with the exception of "A l'Etna") first appeared in my *Tristan Corbière*, part of the Twayne's World Authors Series. Nearly half of these appeared as partial translations and have since been expanded to versions of the entire original texts; since then, too, the translations of *all* the poems have been significantly reworked and refined. The parts that have not been altered, however, were copyrighted in 1979 by Twayne Publishers, Inc., and are here reprinted with the permission of Twayne Publishers, a Division of G.K. Hall and Co., Boston. The poems of Paul Valéry are reproduced by kind permission of the copyright holders, Editions Gallimard, Paris.

My understanding and appreciation of Mallarmé and Valéry, and of the process of translation, owe a great deal to many hours of discussion and correspondence with Ursula Franklin and Enid Rhodes Peschel, respectively. My thanks to them too for their always steadfast friendship and support.

I should, above all, like to express my affection and gratitude first to Henri Peyre, who, to this venture as to others, has so generously given his time and encouragement and from whose advice on usage and the subtle nuances of the French language I have so greatly profited; and to Stephen Mitchell, whose poetic sensitivity and creative energy have long been models to emulate and whose numerous insightful suggestions concerning various problems during the final stages of my work have proven invaluable.

For Ben and Edie Charnas

CONTENTS

INTRODUCTION

A prime motivation behind my undertaking and fabricating the translations that follow was a common, simple one: to improve on those that have preceded. But the title of this volume will, I hope, suggest that this is not intended as just another anthology of translations: with the substitution of "preservations" for "translations" and a lengthy "commentary" section that represents a deviation from normative practice, I have tried to endow the book with a new spirit, a new perspective.

The format consists of a selection of ten poems apiece by Tristan Corbière, Stéphane Mallarmé, and Paul Valéry, with facing English translations. The poems selected are all more or less typical of the three poets in regard to theme and style. They are also relatively short in length, which I have found to be more appropriate to my format: this, unfortunately, eliminates the inclusion of such appealing and demanding poems as Corbière's "Le Poète contumace" and "Litanie du sommeil"; Mallarmé's "L'Après-midi d'un faune" and "Prose (pour des Esseintes)"; and Valéry's "Fragments du Narcisse" and "Le Cimetière marin." Following these texts is a second section entitled "Commentary." Here, each poem will first be paraphrased or otherwise "explained," solely for the orientation of the reader. As some of the poems, particularly Mallarmé's, are so complex or ambiguous that they resist such "résumés" (which are, in these cases, meaningless reductions), the reader not completely familiar with them should consult the brief selected bibliography at the conclusion of the book for more precise analysis of "plot." This brief prefatory explanation will be followed by a detailed discussion of the poem in question that will focus on tone, esthetic intent, ambiguity, imagery, word choice, sonority, syntax, rhythm, rhyme, etc.—in short, on those elements

1

that present specific problems in reading and (thus) in translation and that require critical elucidation. Before proceeding to the poems themselves, and because this new format necessitates some discussion, I should first clarify certain problems concerning the translation of poetry (heretofore implicit: the French-to-English branch of the greater tree); my own conception of it as a *critical art* (and the concept of "preservation"); and the choice of both the format of the volume and of the three poets whose verse (pre)occupies its pages.

In order to appreciate my approach to the translation of these three difficult poets, the reader should first consider two essential, related questions: "what is the ultimate purpose of translations of verse poetry?" and "why read them?"

Translators' (Traditional) Motives

The two most common approaches to the translation of verse poems—the traditional dichotomy of *Übertragung* and *Nach-dichtung*—stand at opposite poles. On the one hand, there are those translators—the vast majority, in fact—who play the role of good Samaritan by paraphrasing or otherwise simplifying the original texts. Their goal is to clarify the basic meaning (although most good poems do not "mean" at all, in the normal sense) for the average reader, and the renderings are often in prose or in prosaic rhymed verse. The motive behind these functional products is well-meaning but commercial: to perform a public service, to make the original texts accessible to a wide audience, to facilitate difficulty, to replace vagueness with clarity and metaphor with concrete denotation. Boris Pasternak has euphemistically called the author of these products the "reliable translator."

On the other hand, a number of translators (often poets themselves) are motivated by personal esthetic drives, regarding the original poem as a springboard (or, in both senses, a "pretext") for their own creative urges, rather than as a model for recapturing or reproduction. The translations in these cases are generally free of the "strictures" of the originals, the motive being to surpass the model or at least to divorce the new creation from it. The ultimate goal, then, is not to render the original accessible to the public, but to transform it, to fabricate a brand new poem. It should be noted that most such "lyrical" translations—good as they may be—are inferior to their models (i.e., if the latter are really worth translating to begin with). Among the proponents of this approach are Jackson Mathews ("he [the translator] is obliged to take over, to give a sense of command, to make his creative will felt"); Renato Poggioli (the translation presupposes "both the ideal presence of the original, and its physical absence": for this critic, translation is an act of exorcism or psychological catharsis); Edmund Wilson ("I have always said that the best translations... are those that depart most widely from the originals—that is, if the translator is himself a good poet"); and the eminent American poet Robert Lowell, whose *Imitations*, abandoning the form and stylistic intent of the originals, invite the reader to appreciate not the celebrated original poems, but the original—and sometimes only faintly derivative—poems of Robert Lowell.

Readers' Motives

Why read translations? In the light of the previous discussion, one might posit two hypothetical responses. First, in the case of "paraphrased" translations, a reader may be motivated by simple curiosity. Which is satisfied... simply. Second, in the case of "poetic" versions (particularly when the translator possesses the stature of a Robert Lowell or a Richard Wilbur), a reader may be interested primarily in the poetry of the translator, not the poet translated. But what is available to the reader (whether literary scholar or general reader) who wishes to become acquainted—*well*-acquainted—with the original poems, to be exposed not only to their power and beauty, but also to their problems and complexities, to those elements that *make* them powerful and beautiful, namely, the linguistic subtleties, esthetic strategies, and stylistic devices (e.g., structure, sound, rhythm, imagery) that characterize their very *poiēsis*, or fabrication?

A Third Alternative: The Critical Eye

It is my feeling that for this last, concerned reader, neither of these two traditional modes of translation can really be satisfactory: the prosaic version falsifies the original poem, and the "poetic" rendering tends to abandon it. There is, however, an alternative approach that would leave the original text relatively intact. It is based on the simple premise that in order to make an original poem accessible *in the form in which it was intended and written*, the translator must first carefully analyze and fully understand it and then make the form and intention of his version correspond as closely as possible to it. Subtle, carefully-wrought poems, then, must encourage subtle, carefully-wrought translations. It is neither prejudice against other theories of translation nor any unprovoked abstract, theoretical rumination on my part, but rather the subtle, carefully-wrought poems of Corbière,

Mallarmé, and Valéry, that have determined the genesis and direction of this approach.

I do not, of course, presume to be the only practitioner of this method: most translations based on a deep respect for their models must necessarily follow the same basic guidelines. But I do feel that this particular approach ought to be articulated in some detail. (Vladimir Nabokov, a devout practitioner, terms it "literal" translation and spends several pages discussing its problems; see Vladimir Nabokov, trans., *Eugene Onegin*, by Aleksandr Pushkin [New York: Pantheon, 1964], I, viii-xi.) To begin with, the answer to the question "why translate?" is exegetical: to understand, appreciate, and question more deeply the original poems. Concerning the problem of the reader of verse translation, the motive of my approach is heuristic: the results of my work ("preservations" and commentary) may help the reader (*and* the translator) discover the mysteries, and learn about the subtleties, of the poems considered here.

It is thus my firm belief that—in the context of this consideration of the motivation of the translator and the needs of the serious reader— the translator's eye should be a *critical* one above all. A "poetic" one as well, to be sure (ultimate decisions concerning the closest equivalent English word choices, rhyme, rhythm, syntax, etc., do require sensitivity and intuitive judgment), but not before careful critical activity has transpired. This demands that he first come to grips with the original text in its entirety, that he familiarize himself with its essential features—linguistic, sonant, rhythmic, etc.—and based on this critical scrutiny make decisions regarding what must be retained in his version and what may be sacrificed with relative impunity. He must also first understand the total context of the poem: the relationship of all of its parts; the relative importance of elements like syntax, grammar, connotation, and polyvalency—in short, the dynamics of the poem to be translated. If all this is not considered, it is certain that—as a result of ignorance, laziness, guess-work, flights of fantasy, indifference, or the like—the original will either be partially lost or totally undermined. These critical processes of scrutiny, selection, and sacrifice are—and should be—parallel to those practiced by the poet; if they are followed assiduously, the crucial problem of the differences between the two languages—the problem of searching for and finding equivalences—may be minimized, if not to a great extent resolved.

Further, the nature of the particular poem to be translated is essential in determining the critical activity that produces the polished version. At one extreme of the poetic spectrum is the limerick, which tells a story and rhymes, usually dispensing with the process of *poiēsis*. At the other is the complex, carefully-written lyric poem. From these antipodal examples, one may posit a corollary, namely, that the less demanding the reading of the original poem is, the more liberties may be taken with it in the translation, for there is, after all, far less to be "lost." A text in which "meaning" represents all that needs to be "carried over" may easily be superseded by an innovative new text that surpasses its basically unimaginative model. But with poems (like those I have selected for this volume) that present problems and challenges to the reader, the faithful translation should not set out to take liberties with or to improve the original, but rather should offer to the reader an intimately similar version of the original poetic experience.

A related aspect of this problem is the accessibility of difficult poems to both the serious general reader and the literary scholar. (I should note that inherent in my approach is the belief that the heuristic consequences of the discussion of the process and problems of translation may not only be useful to the general reader but can also be a potentially important exegetic tool for scholars of French poetry.) I have implied above that accessibility should be a primary consideration of the translator of good poetry. But a second, essential question should now be posed: "*what* is being made accessible?" It seems to me that the critical eye of the translator, if it is used with patience and respect for the original text, may at best ensure that what is being made accessible is not a simplification or a facilitation (falsification) of the original—for the purpose of "making a foreign language easier"—but rather the closest possible reproduction of it, so that the English reader (in the present case) is not cheated and may be allowed to gain a deeper—and unadulterated—understanding of these difficult poems.

Preservations?

Partisans of the "polar" approaches to translation mentioned above base their versions on surrender—on the impossibility of true, faithful translation, because of the insurmountable divergencies of the two languages involved. I would agree with the unstartling position that *absolute* reproduction is impossible, but not with the attitudes betrayed by these methods; for if translation has a responsibility to both the original poets and the readers wishing to become familiar (or more familiar) with their poetry, why relinquish the *effort to approach* such an ideal, faithful rendering? The implications of this question have been a constant motivating factor behind the writing of this book.

Fidelity to the text requires precisely that element which drives good poets to writing in the first place—*patience*, in the Valéryan sense of suffering, slow maturation, and care.

In the Introduction to a collection of translations entitled *The Poem Itself*, Stanley Burnshaw dangles an implicit challenge before all translators of verse poems: "English versions of foreign writings abound, but the reader who wants to experience the poetry of other literatures must look elsewhere; the vast stock of verse translations provides no answer." The first reason he provides is that "a verse translation offers an experience in *English* poetry. It takes the reader away from the foreign literature and into his own, away from the original and into something different." True as this may seem literally, it invites the conclusion that the original can never be preserved and that even the skillful translator can never really hope to approach successful (faithful) retrieval. If I believed this were so, I would continue no further (and in fact, would never have contemplated the writing of this book in the first place).

I should prefer to take up the challenge of attempting to keep intact original poems of high quality, as far as that is possible, given the admitted intrinsic differences between the two languages involved. The process of translation I am advocating here should more accurately be referred to as "preservation," and not translation, to emphasize the fidelity to the original text rather than the disparities between the two languages. Nor imitation, which also admits a certain inherent failure in the enterprise itself. The word suggests, for one thing, a rebuttal to the fallacy of the well-known Italian pun, *traditore/ traduttore*: the translator need not betray the text he is translating, nor must he submit, without a fight, to Robert Frost's quip about poetry's being what is lost in translation. Moreover, "preservation" is a *mot-valise*, containing not only "preserve" (the text), but "reserve" (a rightful place for the original poet) and "serve" (the reader desiring to gain access to the language of poetry).

Verse translations are so difficult because so many simultaneous elements have to be studied, considered, and judged regarding assimilation or rejection, appropriate equivalences or substitutions, and the like. The critical and poetic art of preserving the original text from contamination by the potential inappropriateness of the second language requires a painstaking and uncompromising search for near-correspondence. The specific problems encountered in this endeavor are too numerous to recount here, and many of them will be discussed in detail in the "Commentary" section of this volume. But in general, in order to maintain or preserve the integrity of the original poem, the translator must encounter and attempt to resolve problems that may be, for example, lexical (colloquialisms and neologisms, ambiguity, connotation, puns and other types of word play, etymology, ungrammaticality, hidden words, etc.); syntactical (inversion, disjunction, tmesis, anteposed/postposed adjectives); or sonant (alliteration, assonance, consonance, cacophony, onomatopoeia).

At times, the results of these preservations may seem somewhat "stiff" or "stilted" (especially to the grammatical- or literal-minded reader). This not only cannot be helped, but *should* not be; for in these cases (the four most obvious instances are ellipses, displaced syntax, inversions—noun/adjective, noun/possessive, noun/verb, etc.—and the *appropriate* choice of cognates), the motive is always to respect the original poem, and employing "good" or "normal" or "correct" or "flowing" English (although desirable in prose perhaps) may frequently result in a "nice," "readable" translation, but in an unfortunate undermining or even destruction of the intent, effect, or tone of the original as well. Nabokov eloquently warns against this danger (*Onegin*, p. ix):

> I have been always amused by the stereotyped compliment that a reviewer pays the author of a "new translation." He says: "It reads smoothly." In other words, the hack who has never read the original, and does not know its language, praises an imitation as readable because easy platitudes have replaced in it the intricacies of which he is unaware. "Readable," indeed! A schoolboy's boner mocks the ancient masterpiece less than does its commercial poetization, and it is when the translator sets out to render the "spirit," and not the mere sense of the text, that he begins to traduce his author.

A word about sacrifice involved in the act of preserving poetry is in order. Besides the obvious frustrations of maintaining connotative power and ambiguity and of finding equivalents for certain expressions or locutions in one language that do not exist in the other, there are sacrifices that must be made regarding two aspects of the verse poem inexorably different from language to language: rhyme and versification. Rhyme *must* be retained, for obvious reasons, but it is important to decide in which poems it is among the most urgent stylistic elements, and in which poems it is less essential to preserve completely. In the former instances, I have even at times selected more difficult (even arbitrary) rhymes that attempt to retain the flavor and sonorous character of the originals, at the risk of seeming (in English) forced or even "silly." Examples (to be discussed in the "Commentary" section) are Mallarmé's "erases"/"literasure" (*"Toute l'âme résumée…"*) and Valéry's "lets you aerate"/"literary" and "if y'are"/"afar" ("Valvins"). In the latter cases, rhyme that is *riche* or *suffisante* may be replaced by off-rhyme or consonant-rhyme (or rhyme schemes may be altered) in the interest of preserving something more important, such as a particular linguistic nuance. An example of this sacrifice, taken from one of my Mallarmé versions, is "frigid"/"Cygnet" (*"Le vierge, le vivace et le bel aujourd'hui…"*). (Once again, the "Commentary" section should be consulted for a detailed discussion.) Rhyme is, in fact, too often the major focus of the translator's efforts, and too much is frequently sacrificed to it, particularly in the instance of the translator who, for rhyme's sake, continually adds or subtracts words at will (cf.—in another context!—Verlaine's "O qui dira les torts de la Rime?"). Conserving rhyme and remaining faithful to the other elements of the original may well be the translator's greatest challenge, even if it is, as Nabokov suggests, "mathematically impossible" (*Onegin*, p. ix). Versification is an equally stubborn problem, since the rhythmic methods of measuring verses of poetry differ so brutally between French (syllables) and English (metrical feet). As there is little correspondence between the two systems, I have generally (but by no means always) chosen, in the preservations to follow, to replace the two most common types of French verses (alexandrine, octosyllable) with their closest English rhythmic equivalents (tetrameter, trimeter).

Commentary?

Because the format of this book departs from tradition, some justification of the "Commentary" section is necessary. The key concept here is *accountability*. The immediate, obvious criticism of such a format is that there should be no need to explain or defend translations. But if one accepts the contention that the concept of "preservation" has as its basis a critical method, he will agree that it is essential for the translator to account for his final product. Can a translation stand on its own? The answer to this often-asked question may be "yes," in the case of the "poetic" translation that severs the umbilical link between itself and its model. But in the case of the "preservation," where the motive is critical—to penetrate into the life of the original poem, to communicate, intact, its expressive vitality and stylistic idiosyncrasies to a variety of readers—the actual discussion of choices, rejections, and strategies of both the poets themselves and the translator as well can elucidate these very textual problems and help answer (and, in many instances, pose) questions that the poems elicit. Translating is, after all, not the equivalent of writing poetry, but a subsidiary art. The poet is not obliged to explain his choices or his creative method (although there are often clues found in marginal notes of manuscripts, and poets like Valéry have written voluminously on the process of writing). Conversely, if translating has, as I believe it does, a critical function for its readers, the translator, like the literary critic, has an obligation to share the results of his many hours of reading, analyzing, and consequent choice-making.

Corbière, Mallarmé, Valéry: Why?

As with the format chosen for this book, unorthodoxy must be accounted for once again: because these three poets are not generally included together in anthologies (much less juxtaposed in a cozy troika), I should explain my unlikely selection of them for this volume. Traditionally, the three have been categorized differently: Corbière is, to begin with, uncategorized, a rebel, a thorn in the side of traditional French verse, not to be trusted, and, in fact, never (until recently) taken seriously enough to be granted a place among the important poets or even to be included with them in volumes such as the present one; Mallarmé is usually placed alongside Baudelaire, Rimbaud, and Verlaine, under the rubric of "Symbolist" poets (I have serious reservations concerning this sort of literary-historical pigeonholing); and Valéry is generally considered a "post-Symbolist," often associated with non-French poets such as Yeats, George, and Rilke. Corbière and Mallarmé, it is true, were linked (along with Rimbaud) by Verlaine in his 1883 essay entitled "Les Poètes maudits." But since then, the two have parted company: Corbière's star (dim to begin with) has begun to rise only very recently, while Mallarmé's still shines brightly in the critical heavens. And Mallarmé and Valéry are, of course, often associated as a "master-protégé" pair, although the poetic methods of the two differ more than is commonly acknowledged. But there is no precedent for the inclusion of these three ostensibly incompatible poets together and by themselves in a single volume.

The reasons behind my choice are actually rather apparent, if personalities, "movements," and traditional historical perspectives are abandoned as criteria for conjunction and *poetry* alone is considered. In the "modern" (i.e., post-Baudelairean) era of French verse, these are the three who (along with Rimbaud and various "contemporary" bards) most share a common obsession with the one element that perhaps best characterizes modernity itself: the creative process. All three are poets of the first order (although the excellence of Corbière's verse is most often bypassed or ignored) who wrote in rhymed verse and with consummate care, control, and subtlety. They are three of the most exciting linguistic technicians of the word and—a prime motive behind my selection of them here—unquestionably among the most challenging to preserve in English. Although many of their poetic themes differ, they were all interested in the life of the poetic word; in poems about poetry and the poetic process; in the deception of the careless reader, linguistic games and puzzles, and the subtlety of word combinations; in ambiguity and the polyvalent expression charged with high connotative power; in paradox and conflict; in sounds and the musical properties of word sequences (in Corbière's verse, the music is "discordant," emanating from the Breton hurdy-gurdy and not the seven strings of the traditional poetic lyre); and, above all, in the self-consciousness and the autonomous affirmation of the poetic text.

Besides this poetic element that they share, there is, secondarily, a certain historical logic in linking the three together. The most significant period in the evolution of French poetry was without question the years between the 1860s and the 1920s, during which the revolt against traditional rules of prosody and ossified poetic expression was at its height. Corbière represents (with Baudelaire and Rimbaud) the nineteenth-century break with tradition and the forging of a new poetic perspective; Mallarmé takes poetry out of the nineteenth century (he died two years before *it* did) and into the twentieth; and Valéry is, in the twentieth century, the embodiment of the concept of "pure poetry." The three poets, whose lives overlapped chronologically, make strange bedfellows indeed; but they are together early and successive baton-passers in the relay race of what we now know as "modern" poetry in France.

Corbière, Mallarmé, Valéry: Who?

The lives of these three poets were relatively uneventful: Corbière was chronically unemployed and sickly; Mallarmé was an English teacher at the *lycée* level; and Valéry spent twenty years meditating, worked in a news agency, and was a public figure in his final years. A very brief presentation of their thematic preoccupations and attitudes toward poetry may, however, be helpful in orienting the reader to the poems selected for inclusion in this book. A complete account is scarcely possible in this Introduction and is, besides, not urgent here; the selected bibliography may be consulted for more detailed information concerning the poets' lives and works.

Tristan Corbière (1845-1875), a Breton denied of the sea-faring life because of ill health (tantamount to a fish out of water...), turned to poetry for self-definition and self-discovery. His point of view and tone were, understandably, ironic—directed, in turn, against humanity at large, French bourgeois society, traditional French poetry, and himself—and revolt was the cornerstone of his poetics. In order to develop his own personal expression, he consistently attempted to obliterate all the prosodic standards of traditional French verse: the typical Corbiérian poem is replete with proliferating punctuation, puns and colloquialisms, irregular stanzaic length, conversational tone, (ostensibly) free image-association, incorrect grammar and spelling, and so on. His major themes are the writing of poetry (in several poems, he speaks about how, in theory, not to write poetry, while subtly presenting, in practice, his own manner of writing), pose and paradox, isolation (poetic, social), heterosexual love (or, more to the point, the absence of it: as in everything else, Tristan was an apparent flop in this domain), his native Brittany, and death.

The concept of "theme" is less applicable to the poetry of Stéphane Mallarmé (1842-1898): he never wrote "about" anything, but rather employed things (usually the most insignificant objects) as pretexts for a far greater poetic preoccupation, which was the "subject" of virtually every poem he wrote—poetic creation and the mysterious vitality of the Word. He never succeeded in writing his ideal "Book" ("le Livre"), the perfect, pure result of his poetic alchemy; but the dense, tantalizingly obscure sonnets and other poems he has handed down to future readers reflect the toil and suffering he endured in order to produce texts in which mystery, suggestiveness, and linguistic imprecision and manipulation replace any possible concrete subject matter. Words became the ashes left after the demolition of the poem and its very subject, to be born again and again, like the Phoenix, in subsequent poems. Like Valéry, Mallarmé believed that the poet's duty was to restore the musical element to the lyric, so that the poem became a group of words that did not express a specific idea, thought, or feeling, but that *suggested* by their musically evocative power. Not surprisingly, the dominant thematic obsessions of this extraordinary poet were the dialectics of absence/presence and sterility/creativity; and his poems may well be described as a strange and unique series of linguistic disappearing acts.

Unlike Mallarmé (although there are many similarities between the two), Paul Valéry (1871-1945) was interested less in the finished product (indeed, he believed that a poem "ends" only by chance: he preferred the mind's constant mobility to the poem's static fixation onto the page) than in the *mental process* of creation. His approach to poetry was basically theoretical, analytical. The major themes appearing in his verse as well as in his theoretical writings include the creative process; the workings of the intellect; the relationship of the latter to sensibility and sensuousness; consciousness and its various stages; the relationship between inspiration ("vers donnés") and fabrication ("vers calculés") in poetry; the life of the mind and the maturation, evolution, and "patience" of the thought process; and the dialectics of anticipation and consummation. For Valéry the poem—that subtle, sensuous combination of words and sounds—was a form of "mental exercise": poetic composition and poem were really one in the same, since the poem represented both activity and object. The *process* of writing the poem defines, *is* the poem itself. (He did not, then, share Mallarmé's obsession with the writing itself, the actual black marks on the white page that were at the same time the written [created] poem and the inevitable marks of impurity preventing the poet from attaining pure, ideal expression.) Although Corbière, Mallarmé, and others would have agreed, in varying degrees, with this concept, it was Valéry who was its most patient practitioner and articulator.

Besides being the object of my continued critical involvement and admiration and of many years of reading, each of these important poets has contributed greatly, by their attitudes toward the poetic process, to the very writing of this book: Corbière, with his daring and rebellion, would have approved of the volume's break with tradition in regard to conception and format; Mallarmé's linguistic obsession and tortuous struggle with the compression and purification of the Word (he never wrote without his dictionary close by) dictated, even inspired the many hours I have spent with MM. Littré, Robert, Roget, and Webster; and I have learned, once again, what Valéry knew all along, namely, that patience and its etymological analogue, suffering, are synonymous necessities of the creative process.

PART I

PRESERVATIONS

TRISTAN CORBIÈRE

ÇA?

Des essais?—Allons donc, je n'ai pas essayé!
Etude?—Fainéant je n'ai jamais pillé.
Volume?—Trop broché pour être relié...
De la copie?—Hélas non, ce n'est pas payé!

Un poëme?—Merci, mais j'ai lavé ma lyre.
Un livre?—...Un livre, encor, est une chose à lire!...
Des papiers?—Non, non, Dieu merci, c'est cousu!
Album?—Ce n'est pas blanc, et c'est trop décousu.

Bouts-rimés?—Par quel bout?...Et ce n'est pas joli!
Un ouvrage?—Ce n'est poli ni repoli.
Chansons?—Je voudrais bien, ô ma petite Muse!...
Passe-temps?—Vous croyez, alors, que ça m'amuse?

—Vers?...vous avez flué des vers...—Non, c'est heurté.
—Ah, vous avez couru l'Originalité?...
—Non...c'est une drôlesse assez drôle,—*de rue*—
Qui court encor, sitôt qu'elle se sent courue.

—Du *chic* pur?—Eh qui me donnera des ficelles!
—Du haut vol? Du haut-mal?—Pas de râle, ni d'ailes!
—Chose à mettre à la porte?—...Ou dans une maison
De tolérance.—Ou bien de correction?—Mais non!

—Bon, ce n'est pas classique?—à peine est-ce français!
—Amateur?—Ai-je l'air d'un monsieur à succès?
Est-ce vieux?—Ça n'a pas quarante ans de service...
Est-ce jeune?—Avec l'âge, on guérit de ce vice.

...ÇA c'est naïvement une impudente *pose*;
C'est, ou ce n'est pas *ça*: rien ou quelque chose...
—Un chef-d'œuvre?—Il se peut: je n'en ai jamais fait.
—Mais, est-ce du huron, du Gagne, ou du Musset?

—C'est du...mais j'ai mis là mon humble nom d'auteur,
Et mon enfant n'a pas même un titre menteur.
C'est un coup de raccroc, juste ou faux, par hasard...
L'Art ne me connaît pas. Je ne connais pas l'Art.

Préfecture de police, 20 mai 1873

TRISTAN CORBIÈRE

THAT?

What?...
SHAKESPEARE.

Essays?—Come on, I haven't tried!
Study?—Too lazy to be a crook.
Volume?—Too pasted to be a bound book...
Copy?—No, alas, it's not subsidized!

Poem?—Thanks, but I've hocked my reed.
Book?—...A book, that's still something to read!...
Papers?—No, no, thank God, they're sewn!
Album?—It's not blank, and it's too wind-blown.

End-rhymes?—Which end?...And it shows no craft!
Work?—I never get past the first draft.
Songs?—I'd *love* to, O my darling Muse!...
Pastime?—So you think it keeps me amused?

—Verses?...Something flowing...—No, it's jerky.
—Ah, so you've pursued Originality?...
—No...she's a trull rather droll,—*from the neighborhood*—
Who flees with her purse when she's being pursued.

—Pure *chic*?—Hey, who'll give me the strings!
—High flight? High-fit?—No rasping, nor wings!
—Thing to throw out the door?—...Or into a house
Of ill repute.—Or even detention?—That's close!

—So, it's not classical?—it's barely native!
—Amateur?—Do I look like a guy who's made it?
Is it old?—That doesn't have forty years service...
Is it young?—With age, you can be cured of that vice.

...THAT's naively an impudent *pose*;
It's, or it isn't *that*: nothing, something, who knows?...
—Masterpiece?—Could be: but that's foreign to me.
—But, could it be Huron, or Gagne, or Musset?

—It's...but there I've signed my humble pen-name,
And my child hasn't even a false title to blame.
It's a stroke of luck, right or wrong, miss or hit...
Art doesn't know me. I don't know it.

Police station, May 20, 1873

15

ÉPITAPHE

Il se tua d'ardeur, ou mourut de paresse.
S'il vit, c'est par oubli; voici ce qu'il se laisse:

—Son seul regret fut de n'être pas sa maîtresse.—

Il ne naquit par aucun bout,
Fut toujours poussé vent-de-bout,
Et fut un arlequin-ragoût,
Mélange adultère de tout.

Du *je-ne-sais-quoi*.—Mais ne sachant où;
De l'or,—mais avec pas le sou;
Des nerfs,—sans nerf. Vigueur sans force;
De l'élan,—avec une entorse;
De l'âme,—et pas de violon;
De l'amour,—mais pire étalon.
—Trop de noms pour avoir un nom.—

Coureur d'idéal,—sans idée;
Rime riche,—et jamais rimée;
Sans avoir été,—revenu;
Se retrouvant partout perdu.

Poète, en dépit de ses vers;
Artiste sans art,—à l'envers,
Philosophe,—à tort à travers.

Un drôle sérieux,—pas drôle.
Acteur, il ne sut pas son rôle;
Peintre: il jouait de la musette;
Et musicien: de la palette.

Une tête!—mais pas de tête;
Trop fou pour savoir être bête;
Prenant pour un trait le mot *très*.
—Ses vers faux furent ses seuls vrais.

Oiseau rare—et de pacotille;
Très mâle...et quelquefois très *fille*:
Capable de tout,—bon à rien;

EPITAPH

A suicide from ardor, or died from being lazy.
If he lived, just an oversight; here's his legacy:

—For not being his own mistress alone he feels sorry.—

> He was born at neither end,
> Was always pushed up-wind,
> And was a motley-stew,
> Adulterous concoction too.

> *I-don't-know-what.*—But not knowing where;
> Gold,—but not a penny to spare;
> Nerves,—without nerve. Vigor in vain;
> Verve,—with an ankle sprain;
> Soul,—and his fiddle's a dud;
> Love,—but worst stud.
> —Too many names to have a name.—

> Ideal's pursuer,—no idea in mind;
> *Rime riche,*—and never a rhyme;
> Without having been,—back here;
> Finding himself lost everywhere.

> Poet, in spite of his verse;
> Artist without art,—in reverse,
> Philosopher,—without rhyme or worse.

> A serious comic,—not droll.
> Actor, he didn't know his role;
> Painter: he played the musette;
> And musician: he played the palette.

> A mind!—but never mind;
> Too mad to be asinine;
> Taking as a trait the word *très.*
> His false verses alone were true.

> Rare bird—and second class;
> Very male...and sometimes very *lass*:
> All-capable,—good-for-nil;

Gâchant bien le mal, mal le bien.
Prodigue comme était l'enfant
Du Testament,—sans testament.
Brave, et souvent, par peur du plat,
Mettant ses deux pieds dans le plat.

Coloriste enragé,—mais blême;
Incompris...—surtout de lui-même;
Il pleura, chanta juste faux;
—Et fut un défaut sans défauts.

Ne fut *quelqu'un*, ni quelque chose
Son naturel était la *pose*.
Pas poseur,—posant pour *l'unique*;
Trop naïf, étant trop cynique;
Ne croyant à rien, croyant tout.
—Son goût était dans le dégoût.

Trop cru,—parce qu'il fut trop cuit,
Ressemblant à rien moins qu'à lui,
Il s'amusa de son ennui,
Jusqu'à s'en réveiller la nuit.
Flâneur au large,—à la dérive,
Epave qui jamais n'arrive...

Trop *Soi* pour se pouvoir souffrir,
L'esprit à sec et la tête ivre,
Fini, mais ne sachant finir,
Il mourut en s'attendant vivre
Et vécut, s'attendant mourir.

Ci-gît,—cœur sans cœur, mal planté,
Trop réussi,—comme *raté*.

Messing up good badly, bad well.
Prodigal like the son
Of the Testament,—a will? he had none.
Brave, and often, fearing the trite,
Putting his feet in his bite.

Mad colorist,—but dim;
Misunderstood...—especially by him;
He cried, sang just false;
—And was a fault without faults.

Was neither *someone*, nor something
He was a natural at *posing*.
Not poser,—posing as *unique*;
Too naive, being too much a cynic;
Believing all, believing in nothing.
He found gusto in the disgusting.

Too raw,—because he was too fried,
Resembling nothing less than him inside,
His ennui he had fun keeping:
It even kept him from sleeping.
Adrift on the seas,—without tack,
Wreck that never comes back...

Too *Himself* to be able to stand it,
Dry-dock mind and drunken head,
Finished, not knowing how to end it,
Expecting to live, he died instead
And lived, expecting to be dead.

Here lies,—heartless heart, ill set,
Succeeded too much,—as a *bust*.

I SONNET

AVEC LA MANIÈRE DE S'EN SERVIR

Réglons notre papier et formons bien nos lettres:

Vers filés à la main et d'un pied uniforme,
Emboîtant bien le pas, par quatre en peloton;
Qu'en marquant la césure, un des quatre s'endorme...
Ça peut dormir debout comme soldats de plomb.

Sur le *railway* du Pinde est la ligne, la forme;
Aux fils du télégraphe:—on en suit quatre, en long;
A chaque pieu, la rime—exemple: *chloroforme*.
—Chaque vers est un fil, et la rime un jalon.

—Télégramme sacré—20 mots.—Vite à mon aide...
(Sonnet—c'est un sonnet—) ô Muse d'Archimède!
—La preuve d'un sonnet est par l'addition:

—Je pose 4 et 4 = 8! Alors je procède,
En posant 3 et 3!—Tenons Pégase raide:
"O lyre! O délire! O..."—Sonnet—Attention!

Pic de la Maladetta.—Août.

I SONNET

WITH INSTRUCTIONS FOR USE

Let's put our paper in order and form our letters properly:

Lines hand-wired and of uniform feet,
In perfect box-step, four in a bunch;
If, in marking the pause, one should go out to lunch...
Like lead soldiers standing it may fall asleep.

On the Pindus railway is the line, the form;
On telegraph wires:—we follow four, sprawled out;
At each berth, the rhyme—example: *chloroform*.
—Each verse is a wire, and the rhyme marks the route.

—Sacred telegram—20 words.—Quick, give me some clues...
(Sonnet—it's a sonnet—) O Archimedes' Muse!
—The proof of a sonnet is by addition:

—I add 4 and 4 = 8! Then I proceed,
Adding 3 and 3!—Let's corral that wingèd steed:
"O lyre! O delyrium! O..."—Sonnet—Attention!

Maladetta's Peak.—August.

BONNE FORTUNE ET FORTUNE

Odor della feminità.

Moi, je fais mon trottoir, quand la nature est belle,
Pour la passante qui, d'un petit air vainqueur,
Voudra bien crocheter, du bout de son ombrelle,
Un clin de ma prunelle ou la peau de mon cœur...

Et je me crois content—pas trop!—mais il faut vivre:
Pour promener un peu sa faim, le gueux s'enivre...

Un beau jour—quel métier!—je faisais, comme ça,
Ma croisière.—Métier!...—Enfin, Elle passa
—Elle qui?—La Passante! Elle, avec son ombrelle!
Vrai valet de bourreau, je la frôlai...—mais Elle

Me regarda tout bas, souriant en dessous,
Et...me tendit sa main, et...

                            m'a donné deux sous.

                                Rue des Martyrs.

GOOD LUCK AND LUCK

Odor della feminità.

I walk the streets, when the weather's nice,
For the passer-by who, playing the triumphant part,
With the tip of her parasol will wish to force
A wink from my eye or the skin from my heart...

And I think I'm content—not too much!—but to live longer:
The beggar gets drunk, just to lead on his hunger...

One fine day—what a trade!—I was, like that, cruising
Along.—Trade!...—At last, she came passing
By—Which She?—The Passer-by! She, with her parasol!
Real hangman's valet, I brushed her...—but that Doll

Looked down at me, thinking to herself it was funny,
And...offered her hand to me, and...

                                        gave me two pennies.

                                                Martyrs' St.

A UNE CAMARADE

Que me veux-tu donc, femme trois fois fille?...
Moi qui te croyais un si bon enfant!
—De l'amour?...—Allons: cherche, apporte, pille!
M'aimer aussi, toi!...moi qui t'aimais tant.

Oh! je t'aimais comme...un lézard qui pèle
Aime le rayon qui cuit son sommeil...
L'Amour entre nous vient battre de l'aile:
—Eh! qu'il s'ôte de devant mon soleil!

Mon amour, à moi, n'aime pas qu'on l'aime;
Mendiant, il a peur d'être écouté...
C'est un lazzarone enfin, un bohème,
Déjeunant de jeûne et de liberté.

—Curiosité, bibelot, bricole?...
C'est possible: il est rare—et c'est son bien—
Mais un bibelot cassé se recolle;
Et lui, décollé, ne vaudra plus rien!...

Va, n'enfonçons pas la porte entr'ouverte
Sur un paradis déjà trop rendu!
Et gardons à la pomme, jadis verte,
Sa peau, sous son fard de fruit défendu.

Que nous sommes-nous donc fait l'un à l'autre?...
—Rien...—Peut-être alors que c'est pour cela;
—Quel a commencé?—Pas moi, bon apôtre!
Après, quel dira: c'est donc tout—voilà!

—Tous les deux, sans doute...—Et toi, sois bien sûre
Que c'est encor moi le plus attrapé:
Car si, par erreur, ou par aventure,
Tu ne me trompais...je serais trompé!

Appelons cela: *l'amitié calmée*;
Puisque l'amour veut mettre son holà.
N'y croyons pas trop, chère mal-aimée...
—C'est toujours trop vrai ces mensonges-là!—

Nous pourrons, au moins, ne pas nous maudire
—Si ça t'est égal—le quart-d'heure après.
Si nous en mourons—ce sera de rire...
Moi qui l'aimais tant ton rire si frais!

TO A PAL

So what do you want of me, woman thrice bitch?...
Me who believed you were such a good Joe!
—Love?...—Come on: bring, loot, search!
Love me too, you!...me who loved you so.

Oh! I loved you like...a lizard who's peeling
Loves the ray that cooks its sleep well-done...
Love between us comes beating its wing:
—Hey! get it away from in front of my sun!

My love doesn't like to be liked;
Beggar, it's afraid of being heard...
It's a joker after all, a low-life,
Breakfasting on fasting and free as a bird.

—Curiosity, bauble, perhaps a token?...
It's possible: it's rare—and that's its strong suit—
But a bauble can be glued if it's broken;
And *it* will be worthless, once it's unglued!...

Hey, let's not shut the half-opened door
On a paradise already too beat!
And let's keep on the apple, once sour,
Its skin, disguised as forbidden fruit.

So what have we done to one another?...
—Nothing...—Well, maybe that's why we're like this;
Which one began it?—Not me, brother!
After, which will say: that's all there is!

Both of us, doubtless...—And you, know in advance
That I'm still the one who's most browbeaten:
For if, by mistake, or maybe by chance,
You didn't cheat on me...I'd feel cheated!

Let's just call it: *friendship untroubled*;
Since love wants to step in between me and you.
Let's not be dupes, dearly mislovèd...
—Those lies are always only-too-true!—

The least we could do is avoid our gall
—If that's O.K. with you—the quarter-hour after.
It would be from laughing—if we die from it all....
I who so loved your so-fresh laughter!

A UNE DEMOISELLE

Pour Piano et Chant.

La dent de ton Erard, râtelier osanore,
Et scie et broie à cru, sous son tic-tac nerveux,
La gamme de tes dents, autre clavier sonore...
Touches qui ne vont pas aux cordes des cheveux!

—Cauchemar de meunier, ta: *Rêverie agile!*
—Grattage, ton: *Premier amour à quatre mains!*
O femme transposée en *Morceau difficile,*
Tes croches sans douleur n'ont pas d'accents humains!

Déchiffre au clavecin cet accord de ma lyre;
Télégraphe à musique, il pourra le traduire:
Cri d'os, dur, sec, qui plaque et casse—Plangorer...

Jamais!—La *clef-de-Sol* n'est pas la clef de l'âme,
La *clef-de-Fa* n'est pas la syllabe de *Femme,*
Et deux *demi-soupirs*...ce n'est pas soupirer.

TO A DAMSEL

For Piano and Voice.

The tooth of your Baldwin, inauthentic denture,
Saws and crunches its plain snappy click-clack air,
The scale of your teeth, other musical adventure...
Keys that don't fit with the strings of your hair!

—Miller's nightmare, your: *Agile Reveries*!
—Scratching, your: *First Love for Four Hands*!
O woman transposed into *Difficult Piece*,
Your sorrowless eighth-notes have no human strands!

Sight-read on the harpsichord this harmony from my lyre;
Telegraph-for-music, become versifier:
Bone-crush, hard, dry, that strikes and cracks—Plangorify...

Never!—*Treble-clef* isn't the soul's key,
Nor is *F* the syllable of *Effeminacy*,
And two *eighth-rests*...don't mean repose and sigh.

RAPSODIE DU SOURD

A Madame D***.

L'homme de l'art lui dit:—Fort bien, restons-en là.
Le traitement est fait: vous êtes sourd. Voilà
Comme quoi vous avez l'organe bien perdu.—
Et lui comprit trop bien, n'ayant pas entendu.

—"Eh bien, merci Monsieur, vous qui daignez me rendre
⠀⠀⠀La tête comme un bon cercueil.
Désormais, à crédit, je pourrai tout entendre
⠀⠀⠀Avec un légitime orgueil...

A l'œil—mais gare à l'œil jaloux, gardant la place
De l'oreille au clou!...—Non—A quoi sert de braver?
...Si j'ai sifflé trop haut le ridicule en face,
En face, et bassement, il pourra me baver!...

Moi, mannequin muet, à fil banal!—Demain,
Dans la rue, un ami peut me prendre la main,
En me disant: vieux pot..., ou rien, en radouci;
Et je lui répondrai—Pas mal et vous, merci!—

Si l'un me corne un mot, j'enrage de l'entendre;
Si quelqu'autre se tait: serait-ce par pitié?...
Toujours, comme un *rebus*, je travaille à surprendre
Un mot de travers...—Non—On m'a donc oublié!

—Ou bien—autre guitare—un officieux être
Dont la lippe me fait le mouvement de paître,
Croit me parler...Et moi je tire, en me rongeant,
Un sourire idiot—d'un air intelligent!

—Bonnet de laine grise enfoncé sur mon âme!
Et—coup de pied de l'âne...Hue!—Une bonne-femme
Vieille Limonadière, aussi, de la Passion!
Peut venir saliver sa sainte compassion
Dans ma *trompe-d'Eustache*, à pleins cris, à plein cor,
Sans que je puisse au moins lui marcher sur un cor!

—Bête comme une vierge et fier comme un lépreux,
Je suis là, mais absent...On dit: Est-ce un gâteux,
Poète muselé, hérisson à rebours?...—
Un haussement d'épaule, et ça veut dire: un sourd.

DEAF-MAN'S RHAPSODY

To Mrs. D***.

The man of art told him:—Good, let's leave it at that.
The treatment is over: you're deaf. That's what
Makes your organ completely nonfunctioning.—
And *he* understood too well, taking in not a thing.

—"Well, Sir, thanks a bunch for making
          My head a nice coffin inside.
Henceforth, on credit, I'll hear everything
          With justifiable pride...

For the eye—But woe to the jealous eye, replacing the
Ear nailed up!...—No—Why persevere?
...If I shouted too loud at the sot facing me,
In my face, and basely, he'd drool insults in my ear!...

I, mute dummy, with banal strings!—On the street,
Tomorrow, a friend could come up and greet
Me, saying: old crock..., or nothing, *sotto*
Voce; and I'd answer him—Not bad, thanks, and you!—

If one trumpets a word, I'm itching to snatch it;
If some other is silent: would it be from pity?...
Always, like a *puzzle*, I'm straining to catch it—
A word gone astray...—No—So they've forgotten me!

—Or else—other guitar—an officious guy whose gesture
With his fat lip looks like he's being put out to pasture,
Thinks he's speaking to me...And *I* put on, from fear,
A vacuous smile—with an intelligent air!

—Grey woolen bonnet thrust onto my soul!
And—ass's kick...Giddyup!—Good-ol'-gal
Old Proprietress, as well, of Passion!
Might come up to slobber her saintly compassion
In my *Eustachian tuba*, blaring, loud as a horn,
Not letting me even step on her corn!

—Silly as a virgin and proud as a leper,
I'm there, but absent...They say: Is he an old dotard,
A muzzled poet, a hedgehog in reverse?...—
A shrug of the shoulders, which means: a deaf person.

—Hystérique tourment d'un Tantale acoustique!
Je vois voler des mots que je ne puis happer;
Gobe-mouche impuissant, mangé par un moustique,
Tête-de turc gratis où chacun peut taper.

O musique céleste: entendre, sur du plâtre,
Gratter un coquillage! un rasoir, un couteau
Grinçant dans un bouchon!...un couplet de théâtre!
Un os vivant qu'on scie! un monsieur! un rondeau!...

—Rien—Je parle sous moi...Des mots qu'à l'air je jette
De chic, et sans savoir si je parle en indou...
Ou peut-être en canard, comme la clarinette
D'un aveugle bouché qui se trompe de trou.

—Va donc, balancier soûl affolé dans ma tête!
Bats en branle ce bon tam-tam, chaudron fêlé
Qui rend la voix de femme ainsi qu'une sonnette,
Qu'un coucou!...quelquefois: un moucheron ailé...

—Va te coucher, mon cœur! et ne bats plus de l'aile.
Dans la lanterne sourde étouffons la chandelle,
Et tout ce qui vibrait là—je ne sais plus où—
Oubliette où l'on vient de tirer le verrou.

—Soyez muette pour moi, contemplative Idole,
Tous les deux, l'un par l'autre, oubliant la parole,
Vous ne me direz mot: je ne répondrai rien...
Et rien ne pourra dédorer l'entretien.

Le silence est d'or (Saint Jean Chrysostome).

—Hysterical torment of an acoustical Tantalus!
I see words fly by that I just can't catch;
Impotent gaper, by mosquitoes eaten up,
Free try-your-strength game where each one gets a smack.

O heavenly music: to hear, on plaster, scrape
The sound of a shell! a razor, a knife go
Grating in a cork!...a theatrical tirade!
A live bone being sawed! a gent! a rondeau!...

—Zilch—I speak beneath me...In the air words I let
Fly *as chic*, unaware if I speak Hindi or not...
Or perhaps it's duck-talk, like the clarinet
Of a closed-minded blindman who strikes the wrong note.

—Go then, smashed balance-wheel gone haywire in my head!
Beat doddering this nice tom-tom, a cauldron cracked
That makes a woman's voice sound like a rattle instead,
Or a cuckoo!...sometimes: like a wingèd gnat...

—Go lie down, my heart! and no more take flight.
In the dark deaf lantern let's put out the light,
And all that was moving—I don't recall where—
Prison, and they've just bolted me there.

—Be mute for me, contemplative Idol,
Both of us, one by the other, voices bridled,
You'll say nothing to me: the same I'll do...
And nothing will tarnish the interview.

Silence is golden (Saint John Golden-Mouth).

A L'ETNA

Sicelides Musæ, paulo majora canamus.

VIRGILE.

Etna—j'ai monté le Vésuve...
Le Vésuve a beaucoup baissé:
J'étais plus chaud que son effluve,
Plus que sa crête hérissé...

—Toi que l'on compare à la femme...
Pourquoi?—Pour ton âge? ou ton âme
De caillou cuit?...—Ça fait rêver...
—Et tu t'en fais rire à crever!—

—Tu ris jaune et tousses: sans doute,
Crachant un vieil amour malsain;
La lave coule sous la croûte
De ton vieux cancer au sein.

—Couchons ensemble, Camarade!
Là—mon flanc sur ton flanc malade:
Nous sommes frères, par Vénus,
Volcan!...
       Un peu moins...un peu plus...

           Palerme.—Août.

TO ETNA

Sicelides Musæ, paulo majora canamus.

VERGIL.

Etna—I've mounted Vesuvius...
Vesuvius has been humping less:
I was hotter than her effluvium,
Bristling more than her crest...

—You whom they cast in a woman's role...
—Why?—For your age? or your soul
Of baked flint?...—That makes me dream...
—And you laugh of it enough to bust a seam!—

—You laugh yellow and cough: no doubt,
Spitting a sickly old love right out;
Lava flows beneath the crust
Of your chronic cancer of the breast.

—Let's hit the sack, Confrere!
My flank on your sick flank—there:
We're brothers, by Venus,
Volcano!...
        A little more...a little less...

Palermo.—August.

PAYSAGE MAUVAIS

Sables de vieux os—Le flot râle
Des glas: crevant bruit sur bruit...
—Palud pâle, où la lune avale
De gros vers, pour passer la nuit.

—Calme de peste, où la fièvre
Cuit...Le follet damné languit.
—Herbe puante où le lièvre
Est un sorcier poltron qui fuit...

—La Lavandière blanche étale
Des trépassés le linge sale,
Au *soleil des loups*...—Les crapauds,

Petits chantres mélancoliques
Empoisonnent de leurs coliques,
Les champignons, leurs escabeaux.

Marais de Guérande.—Avril.

DARK LANDSCAPE

Old bone beaches—the waves' rhonchus
Knells: bursting chime upon chime...
—Wan swamp, where the moon chomps
Giant worms, to pass the nighttime.

—Calm of a plague, where
Fever fries...The cursèd sprite
Wastes.—Stinking grass where the hare
Is a cowardly wizard in flight...

—The white Laundress spreads
The dirty wash of the dead,
Beneath the *wolves' sun*...—The toads,

Little bards melancholic
Poison with their colic,
The mushrooms, their stool-abodes.

Guérande Marsh.—April.

PETIT MORT POUR RIRE

Va vite, léger peigneur de comètes!
Les herbes au vent seront tes cheveux;
De ton œil béant jailliront les feux
Follets, prisonniers dans les pauvres têtes…

Les fleurs de tombeau qu'on nomme Amourettes
Foisonneront plein ton rire terreux…
Et les myosotis, ces fleurs d'oubliettes…

Ne fais pas le lourd: cercueils de poètes
Pour les croque-morts sont de simples jeux,
Boîtes à violon qui sonnent le creux…
Ils te croiront mort—Les bourgeois sont bêtes—
Va vite, léger peigneur de comètes!

HE WAS JEST A CHILD

Fleet comber of comets, speed on by!
The grass in the wind will be your hair;
From your hollow eye will leap wisp-flairs,
Which in wretched heads imprisoned lie...

The funeral flowers they call Love's Sigh
And these dongeon-flowers, the forget-me-ne'er...
Will make your earthy laugh multiply...

Don't play the heavy: poets' coffins, why,
They're simple games for the pallbearers,
Fiddle-boxes with a hollow air...
They'll think you dead—Another bourgeois lie—
Fleet comber of comets, speed on by!

STÉPHANE MALLARMÉ

SALUT

Rien, cette écume, vierge vers
A ne désigner que la coupe;
Telle loin se noie une troupe
De sirènes mainte à l'envers.

Nous naviguons, ô mes divers
Amis, moi déjà sur la poupe
Vous l'avant fastueux qui coupe
Le flot de foudres et d'hivers;

Une ivresse belle m'engage
Sans craindre même son tangage
De porter debout ce salut

Solitude, récif, étoile
A n'importe ce qui valut
Le blanc souci de notre toile.

STÉPHANE MALLARMÉ

TOAST

Ought, this foam, virgin verse
To only the cup
Tell; afar thus drowns a troop
Of sirens myriad inverse.

We sail, O my divers
Friends, I already on the poop
You the festive prow that chops
The tides of thunder and of winters;

A transport calm enlists
Me without fearing even its pitch
To propose standing this toast

Solitude, reef, asterisk
To whatever deserved most
The blank concern of our canvas.

La chevelure vol d'une flamme à l'extrême
Occident de désirs pour la tout déployer
Se pose (je dirais mourir un diadème)
Vers le front couronné son ancien foyer

Mais sans or soupirer que cette vive nue
L'ignition du feu toujours intérieur
Originellement la seule continue
Dans le joyau de l'œil véridique ou rieur

Une nudité de héros tendre diffame
Celle qui ne mouvant astre ni feux au doigt
Rien qu'à simplifier avec gloire la femme
Accomplit par son chef fulgurante l'exploit

De semer de rubis le doute qu'elle écorche
Ainsi qu'une joyeuse et tutélaire torche.

The combèd hair flight of a flame to the far
West of desires to unfurl it all comes
To rest (I would say a dying diadem)
Toward the crowned brow its original hearth

But without gold sigh that this cloud alive
The ignition of the ever inner fire
Originally the sole one persevere
In the jewel of the truthful or laughing eye

A nudity of tender hero defames
Her who moving on her finger not star nor fires' heat
Only to simplify with glory woman with flames
Of lightning achieves by her hed the deed

Of sowing with rubies the doubt she flays
Just like a joyful and tutelary blaze.

SAINTE

A la fenêtre recelant
Le santal vieux qui se dédore
De sa viole étincelant
Jadis avec flûte ou mandore,

Est la Sainte pâle, étalant
Le livre vieux qui se déplie
Du Magnificat ruisselant
Jadis selon vêpre et complie:

A ce vitrage d'ostensoir
Que frôle une harpe par l'Ange
Formée avec son vol du soir
Pour la délicate phalange

Du doigt que, sans le vieux santal
Ni le vieux livre, elle balance
Sur le plumage instrumental,
Musicienne du silence.

SAINT

At the window concealing
The ancient santal gilt no more
Of her viol glowing
With flute or mandola of yore,

Is the pale Saint, revealing
The ancient book opening forth
The Magnificat flowing
For vesper and complin of yore:

At this monstrance windowlight
That brushes by the Angel a harp
Formed with its evening flight
As the delicate tip

Of the finger that, without the agèd
Santal nor the agèd book, she balances
On the instrumental plumage,
Musician of silence.

Quand l'ombre menaça de la fatale loi
Tel vieux Rêve, désir et mal de mes vertèbres,
Affligé de périr sous les plafonds funèbres
Il a ployé son aile indubitable en moi.

Luxe, ô salle d'ébène où, pour séduire un roi
Se tordent dans leur mort des guirlandes célèbres,
Vous n'êtes qu'un orgueil menti par les ténèbres
Aux yeux du solitaire ébloui de sa foi.

Oui, je sais qu'au lointain de cette nuit, la Terre
Jette d'un grand éclat l'insolite mystère,
Sous les siècles hideux qui l'obscurcissent moins.

L'espace à soi pareil qu'il s'accroisse ou se nie
Roule dans cet ennui des feux vils pour témoins
Que s'est d'un astre en fête allumé le génie.

When shadow menaced with its fatal ruling
Such old Dream, desire and ill of my feeling,
Afflicted with perishing beneath funereal ceilings
It has folded in me its indubitable wing.

Splendor, O ebony hall where, to seduce a potentate
Twist in their throes celebrated garlands,
You are but a pride belied by the shades
In the eyes of the solitaire dazzled by his faith.

Yes, I know that afar from this night, the Earth casts
Of a great flash the mystery strange,
Beneath the hideous centuries that obscure it less.

Space equal to itself whether it grow or derange
Rolls in this ennui vile fires as witness
That has from a joyous star been lit genius.

Le vierge, le vivace et le bel aujourd'hui
Va-t-il nous déchirer avec un coup d'aile ivre
Ce lac dur oublié que hante sous le givre
Le transparent glacier des vols qui n'ont pas fui!

Un cygne d'autrefois se souvient que c'est lui
Magnifique mais qui sans espoir se délivre
Pour n'avoir pas chanté la région où vivre
Quand du stérile hiver a resplendi l'ennui.

Tout son col secouera cette blanche agonie
Par l'espace infligé à l'oiseau qui le nie,
Mais non l'horreur du sol où le plumage est pris.

Fantôme qu'à ce lieu son pur éclat assigne,
Il s'immobilise au songe froid de mépris
Que vêt parmi l'exil inutile le Cygne.

The virgin, the enduring and the beauteous today
Will it shear for us with a feverish wing-blast
This hard forgotten lake haunted beneath the frost
By the glacier transparent of flights not flown away!

A swan of old recalls it is he
Magnificent but who hopelessly strives
To escape for not having sung the region to live
When of sterile winter gleamed the ennui.

His whole neck will disannex this agony white
By space inflicted on the bird who denies it, but not
The horror of the ground where the plumage is caught.

Phantom whom to this place his pure glow indicts,
He fixes himself in the dream of scorn, frigid,
That adorns amidst futile exile the Cygnet.

Ses purs ongles très haut dédiant leur onyx,
L'Angoisse, ce minuit, soutient, lampadophore,
Maint rêve vespéral brûlé par le Phénix
Que ne recueille pas de cinéraire amphore

Sur les crédences, au salon vide: nul ptyx,
Aboli bibelot d'inanité sonore,
(Car le Maître est allé puiser des pleurs au Styx
Avec ce seul objet dont le Néant s'honore).

Mais proche la croisée au nord vacante, un or
Agonise selon peut-être le décor
Des licornes ruant du feu contre une nixe,

Elle, défunte nue en le miroir, encor
Que, dans l'oubli fermé par le cadre, se fixe
De scintillations sitôt le septuor.

Its pure nails on high consecrating their onyx,
Anguish, this midnight, bears, lampadephore,
Many a vesperal dream burned by the Phoenix
That gathers up not any cinerary amphora

On the credences, in the empty parlor: no ptyx,
Nullified knickknack of sonorous inanity,
(For the Master went off to draw tears from the Styx
With this sole object honored by Nihility).

But next the casement to the north vacant, a karat
Flickers according to perhaps the decor
Of unicorns hurling fire at a nix,

She, deceased nude into the mirror, whereat,
In the oblivion enclosed by the frame, is fixed
With scintillations so soon the septuor.

LE TOMBEAU DE CHARLES BAUDELAIRE

Le temple enseveli divulgue par la bouche
Sépulcrale d'égout bavant boue et rubis
Abominablement quelque idole Anubis
Tout le museau flambé comme un aboi farouche

Ou que le gaz récent torde la mèche louche
Essuyeuse on le sait des opprobres subis
Il allume hagard un immortel pubis
Dont le vol selon le réverbère découche

Quel feuillage séché dans les cités sans soir
Votif pourra bénir comme elle se rasseoir
Contre le marbre vainement de Baudelaire

Au voile qui la ceint absente avec frissons
Celle son Ombre même un poison tutélaire
Toujours à respirer si nous en périssons.

THE TOMB OF CHARLES BAUDELAIRE

The buried temple divulges by its sepulchral
Sewer-mouth slobbering slop and rubies
Abominably some idol Anubis
Its whole snout aflame like a ferocious yelp

Or the recent gas twist the shady wick as it might
Absorbing as we know endured abuse
It lights haggard an immortal pubis
Whose stealth against the street-lamp hangs out all night

What dried foliage in nightless quarters
Votive could bless as it settle
Against Baudelaire's vainly marble

From the veil that wreathes it absent with shudders
It his very Shade a tutelary poison
Always to be breathed if it destroys us.

Toute l'âme résumée
Quand lente nous l'expirons
Dans plusieurs ronds de fumée
Abolis en autres ronds

Atteste quelque cigare
Brûlant savamment pour peu
Que la cendre se sépare
De son clair baiser de feu

Ainsi le chœur des romances
A la lèvre vole-t-il
Exclus-en si tu commences
Le réel parce que vil

Le sens trop précis rature
Ta vague littérature.

The entire soul summarized
When slow we expire it
In several smoke spirals
In others nullified

Attests some cigar
Burning learnedly if ever
The ash dissevers
From its bright kiss of fire

The chorus of romances hence
To the lip volatiles
Exclude from it if you commence
The real because vile

Too-precise meaning erases
Your vague literasure.

Une dentelle s'abolit
Dans le doute du Jeu suprême
A n'entr'ouvrir comme un blasphème
Qu'absence éternelle de lit.

Cet unanime blanc conflit
D'une guirlande avec la même,
Enfui contre la vitre blême
Flotte plus qu'il n'ensevelit.

Mais, chez qui du rêve se dore
Tristement dort une mandore
Au creux néant musicien

Telle que vers quelque fenêtre
Selon nul ventre que le sien,
Filial on aurait pu naître.

A lace plays dead
In the doubt of the supreme Game
To half-open as profane
But eternal absence of bed.

This conflict consolidated white
Of one garland with the same,
Faded against the pale pane
Floats more than it hides.

But, where dwells of dream the gilder
Sadly sleeps a mandola
With lyric hollow no-tone

Such that toward some window torn
From no belly but its own,
Filial one might have been born.

A la nue accablante tu
Basse de basalte et de laves
A même les échos esclaves
Par une trompe sans vertu

Quel sépulcral naufrage (tu
Le sais, écume, mais y baves)
Suprême une entre les épaves
Abolit le mât dévêtu

Ou cela que furibond faute
De quelque perdition haute
Tout l'abîme vain éployé

Dans le si blanc cheveu qui traîne
Avarement aura noyé
Le flanc enfant d'une sirène.

To the oppressive cloud checked
Base with lava and basalt
Even down to the slavish echoes
By a trump without note

What sepulchral shipwreck (you
Know it, foam, but drool thereat)
One supreme among the residue
Abolished the unclothed mast

Or hid that furious for lack
Of some lofty loss
The whole vain spread abyss

In the so white hair that drags on
Avariciously will have drowned
A siren's infant flank.

PAUL VALÉRY

NAISSANCE DE VÉNUS

De sa profonde mère, encor froide et fumante,
Voici qu'au seuil battu de tempêtes, la chair
Amèrement vomie au soleil par la mer,
Se délivre des diamants de la tourmente.

Son sourire se forme, et suit sur ses bras blancs
Qu'éplore l'orient d'une épaule meurtrie,
De l'humide Thétis la pure pierrerie,
Et sa tresse se fraye un frisson sur ses flancs.

Le frais gravier, qu'arrose et fuit sa course agile,
Croule, creuse rumeur de soif, et le facile
Sable a bu les baisers de ses bonds puérils;

Mais de mille regards ou perfides ou vagues,
Son œil mobile mêle aux éclairs de périls
L'eau riante, et la danse infidèle des vagues.

PAUL VALÉRY

BIRTH OF VENUS

From her profound sea-womb, cold and smoking still,
Now her flesh, at the threshold that tempests beat
Bitterly spewed in the sun by the sea,
Delivers itself from the diamonds of the gale.

Her smile shapes, and pursues against her arms so white
That the slope of a bruised shoulder bewails,
Of bewetted Thetis the pure precious jewels,
And her tress traces for itself a chill on her sides.

The moist gravel, that her agile path sprays and flees,
Spills down, hollow murmur of thirst, and the waiting
Sand has drunk the kisses of her childlike leaps;

But with a thousand gazes either false or vague,
Her restless eye blends with perils' lightning
The smiling water, and the fickle dance of the waves.

AU BOIS DORMANT

La princesse, dans un palais de rose pure,
Sous les murmures, sous la mobile ombre dort,
Et de corail ébauche une parole obscure
Quand les oiseaux perdus mordent ses bagues d'or.

Elle n'écoute ni les gouttes, dans leurs chutes,
Tinter d'un siècle vide au lointain le trésor,
Ni, sur la forêt vague, un vent fondu de flûtes
Déchirer la rumeur d'une phrase de cor.

Laisse, longue, l'écho rendormir la diane,
O toujours plus égale à la molle liane
Qui se balance et bat tes yeux ensevelis.

Si proche de ta joue et si lente la rose
Ne va pas dissiper ce délice de plis
Secrètement sensible au rayon qui s'y pose.

SLEEPING BEAUTY

The princess, in a palace of pure roses,
Beneath whispers and moving shadows is sleeping,
And a word of coral obscurely composes
When wayward birds peck at her golden rings.

She catches neither water's splash, in cascades,
Ring from afar of a lost time the treasure,
Nor a wind diffused by flutes, on the looming woods,
Rend the murmur of a horn's mournful measure.

Let, long, the echo lull reveille,
O more and more like the soft liana
That dangles and brushes your eyes shrouded heavily.

So close to your cheek and so plodding the rose
Is not going to scatter this treasure of folds
Secretly yielding to the rays that lay on it.

VALVINS

Si tu veux dénouer la forêt qui t'aère
Heureuse, tu te fonds aux feuilles, si tu es
Dans la fluide yole à jamais littéraire,
Traînant quelques soleils ardemment situés

Aux blancheurs de son flanc que la Seine caresse
Emue, ou pressentant l'après-midi chanté,
Selon que le grand bois trempe une longue tresse,
Et mélange ta voile au meilleur de l'été.

Mais toujours près de toi que le silence livre
Aux cris multipliés de tout le brut azur,
L'ombre de quelque page éparse d'aucun livre

Tremble, reflet de voile vagabonde sur
La poudreuse peau de la rivière verte
Parmi le long regard de la Seine entr'ouverte.

VALVINS

If you wish to unloose the forest that lets you aerate
Happy, you fade into the leaves, if y'are
In the fluid yawl forever literary,
Trailing several suns ardently placed from afar

On the white of its side that the Seine caresses
Moved, or sounding out the singing of afternoon,
According as the great woods soak their long tresses,
And mingle your sail in summer's paragon.

But always near you whom the silence delivers
To the multiplied calls of the whole brute azure,
The shadow of some page scattered from any book

Trembles, drifting sail's reflection on
The green river's silty skin
Amid the parted Seine's languorous look.

ÉTÉ

A Francis Vielé-Griffin.

Eté, roche d'air pur, et toi, ardente ruche,
O mer! Eparpillée en mille mouches sur
Les touffes d'une chair fraîche comme une cruche,
Et jusque dans la bouche où bourdonne l'azur;

Et toi, maison brûlante, Espace, cher Espace
Tranquille, où l'arbre fume et perd quelques oiseaux,
Où crève infiniment la rumeur de la masse
De la mer, de la marche et des troupes des eaux,

Tonnes d'odeurs, grands ronds par les races heureuses
Sur le golfe qui mange et qui monte au soleil,
Nids purs, écluses d'herbe, ombres des vagues creuses,
Bercez l'enfant ravie en un poreux sommeil!

Dont les jambes (mais l'une est fraîche et se dénoue
De la plus rose), les épaules, le sein dur,
Le bras qui se mélange à l'écumeuse joue
Brillent abandonnés autour du vase obscur

Où filtrent les grands bruits pleins de bêtes puisées
Dans les cages de feuille et les mailles de mer
Par les moulins marins et les huttes rosées
Du jour...Toute la peau dore les treilles d'air.

SUMMER

To Francis Vielé-Griffin.

Summer, rock of sweet air, and you, ardent swarm,
O sea! Scattered in a thousand flies on
The tufts of a flesh fresh as an urn,
And up to the mouth where buzzes the horizon;

And you, burning house, Space, dear Space
Calm, where the tree smokes and lets go several birds,
Where bursts infinitely the murmur of the mass
Of the main, of the march and the waters' herds,

Tuns of smells, great circles by happy races
On the hungry gulf climbing to the sun, pure nests,
Locks of grass, shadows of the hollow waves,
Rock the child entranced in a porous rest!

Whose legs (but one is fresh and comes undone
From the pinker), firm breast, shoulderblades,
Arm that blends with the cheek of foam
Shine forsaken around the obscure vase

Where filter great sounds of beasts drawn up
In cages of leaf and stitches of brine
By maritime mills and rosy huts
Of the day...All her skin gilds the air on its vine.

L'ABEILLE

A Francis de Miomandre.

Quelle, et si fine, et si mortelle,
Que soit ta pointe, blonde abeille,
Je n'ai, sur ma tendre corbeille,
Jeté qu'un songe de dentelle.

Pique du sein la gourde belle,
Sur qui l'Amour meurt ou sommeille,
Qu'un peu de moi-même vermeille
Vienne à la chair ronde et rebelle!

J'ai grand besoin d'un prompt tourment:
Un mal vif et bien terminé
Vaut mieux qu'un supplice dormant!

Soit donc mon sens illuminé
Par cette infime alerte d'or
Sans qui l'Amour meurt ou s'endort!

THE BEE

To Francis de Miomandre.

What, both so fine, and so mortal,
Ever be your barb, blond bee,
I have, on my delicate balcony,
Thrown but a dream of dentelle.

Sting the breast's wondrous flask,
On which Love dies or is slumbering,
That a bit of my bright-red being
Might come to the round and rebellious flesh!

I sorely need a prompt offense:
A sharp and short-lived misery
Is better than sleeping agony!

Let then illumined be my sense
By this tiny golden-raid
Without which Love dies or fades!

LES PAS

Tes pas, enfants de mon silence,
Saintement, lentement placés,
Vers le lit de ma vigilance
Procèdent muets et glacés.

Personne pure, ombre divine,
Qu'ils sont doux, tes pas retenus!
Dieux!...tous les dons que je devine
Viennent à moi sur ces pieds nus!

Si, de tes lèvres avancées,
Tu prépares pour l'apaiser,
A l'habitant de mes pensées
La nourriture d'un baiser,

Ne hâte pas cet acte tendre,
Douceur d'être et de n'être pas,
Car j'ai vécu de vous attendre,
Et mon cœur n'était que vos pas.

STEPS

Your steps, stillborns of my silence,
Sacredly, slowly placed,
Toward the bed of my vigilance
Proceed mute and glazed.

Pure one, divine shade,
Your detained steps, how sweet!
Gods!...every gift I presage
Comes to me on these bare feet!

If, from your proffered lips,
To appease it you are preparing,
For the dweller of my thinking
The sustenance of a kiss,

This tender act do not press,
Sweetness of to be and of not to be,
For I have lived from awaiting thee,
And my heart was but thy steps.

LA DORMEUSE

A Lucien Fabre.

Quels secrets dans son cœur brûle ma jeune amie,
Ame par le doux masque aspirant une fleur?
De quels vains aliments sa naïve chaleur
Fait ce rayonnement d'une femme endormie?

Souffle, songes, silence, invincible accalmie,
Tu triomphes, ô paix plus puissante qu'un pleur,
Quand de ce plein sommeil l'onde grave et l'ampleur
Conspirent sur le sein d'une telle ennemie.

Dormeuse, amas doré d'ombres et d'abandons,
Ton repos redoutable est chargé de tels dons,
O biche avec langueur longue auprès d'une grappe,

Que malgré l'âme absente, occupée aux enfers,
Ta forme au ventre pur qu'un bras fluide drape,
Veille; ta forme veille, et mes yeux sont ouverts.

SLUMBERER

To Lucien Fabre.

What secrets in her heart does my young friend consume,
Soul through her sweet mask aspiring a flower?
From what vain sustenance does her innocent bloom
Make this radiance of a woman in slumber?

Breath, visions, hush, invincible lull,
You triumph, O tranquillity more terrible than a tear,
When from this full sleep the heavy wave and the bulk
Conspire on the breast of such an enemy.

Slumberer, shimmering store of shadows and shifts,
Your redoubtable rest is laden with such gifts,
O dear with long languor by a cluster of grapes,

That despite the absent soul, in hell occupied,
Your pure belly's form that a fluid arm drapes,
Watches; your form watches, and my eyes open wide.

LES GRENADES

Dures grenades entr'ouvertes
Cédant à l'excès de vos grains,
Je crois voir des fronts souverains
Eclatés de leurs découvertes!

Si les soleils par vous subis,
O grenades entre-bâillées,
Vous ont fait d'orgueil travaillées
Craquer les cloisons de rubis,

Et que si l'or sec de l'écorce
A la demande d'une force
Crève en gemmes rouges de jus,

Cette lumineuse rupture
Fait rêver une âme que j'eus
De sa secrète architecture.

POMEGRENADES

Firm pomegrenades gaping
Yielding to the excess of your seeds,
Sovereign brows I think I see
Burst from their uncoverings!

If the suns by you endured,
O pomegrenades half-cleft,
Have made you with pride inured
Crack your ruby septa,

And...and if the dried gold of the rind
At the request of a force
Bursts in magenta gems of juice,

This luminous rupture
Makes my former mind
Dream of its secret architecture.

LA CARESSE

Mes chaudes mains, baigne-les
Dans les tiennes…Rien ne calme
Comme d'amour ondulés
Les passages d'une palme.

Tout familiers qu'ils me sont,
Tes anneaux à longues pierres
Se fondent dans le frisson
Qui fait clore les paupières

Et le mal s'étale, tant,
Comme une dalle est polie,
Une caresse l'étend
Jusqu'à la mélancolie.

CARESS

My warm hands, let them bathe
In yours...Nothing can calm
Like with love waved
The passings of a palm.

As I know them still,
Your links with long stones
Are melting in the thrill
That makes my eyes close

And dread spreads, such,
As a slab is smoothed,
A caress makes it stretch
To melancholy soothed.

NEIGE

Quel silence, battu d'un simple bruit de bêche!…

Je m'éveille, attendu par cette neige fraîche
Qui me saisit au creux de ma chère chaleur.
Mes yeux trouvent un jour d'une dure pâleur
Et ma chair langoureuse a peur de l'innocence.
Oh! combien de flocons, pendant ma douce absence,
Durent les sombres cieux perdre toute la nuit!
Quel pur désert tombé des ténèbres sans bruit
Vint effacer les traits de la terre enchantée
Sous cette ample candeur sourdement augmentée
Et la fondre en un lieu sans visage et sans voix,
Où le regard perdu relève quelques toits
Qui cachent leur trésor de vie accoutumée
A peine offrant le vœu d'une vague fumée.

SNOW

What silence, transmuted by a sole spade's blow!...

I awake, awaited by this new snow
That seizes me in the hollow of my wondrous warmth.
My eyes find a day of bleakness harsh
And my languorous flesh fears innocence.
Oh! how many flakes, during my sweet absence,
Must the somber skies all night have endured to lose!
What pure desert fallen noiselessly from the shades
Came to blot out the enchanted earth's trace
Beneath this ample candor secretly increased
And melt it to a faceless, voiceless spot,
Where the lost look reconstructs a few roofs that
Conceal their treasure of life awoke
Hardly offering the vow of a vague wisp of smoke.

PART II
COMMENTARY

TRISTAN CORBIÈRE

ÇA?

This liminal poem of *Les Amours jaunes* is prototypically Corbiérian: in the process of belittling himself as a poet unconcerned with poetry in its traditional, formal sense and of failing to categorize his verse within one of the conventional, recognizable forms (as announced by the self-deprecating title), the poet in fact creates a text that breaks with tradition and represents an innovative demonstration of idiosyncratic technique. As in "Epitaphe" (to be studied presently), the propositions set forth in the first part of almost every verse are constantly undermined in the second. According to the literal meanings of the "responses" of the first four stanzas, Corbière's verse is devoid of effort, has no roots in tradition, is carelessly edited, unsubsidized, unlyrical, unreadable, unattached, incoherent, inchoate, unpolished, unmusical, unamusing, unoriginal. But this poem is much more than a simple exercise in frustration or masochism: the pose of "nonpoet" is itself undercut by a new poetics based precisely on the absence of rhetorical language. (The title—neutering the poetry itself—and the epigraph, quoting one of the Bard's least eloquent and recognizable pronouncements, attest to this.) This new manner of expression is characterized by an informal, conversational tone, colloquial expressions, accumulation, spontaneity, irregular versification (syllable count varies, due to a willfully perverse and arbitrary usage of silent *e*'s and dieresis), constant puns and word play, and aberrant punctuation (the poem contains thirty-four dashes, thirty-one question marks, twenty-seven commas, fifteen ellipses, ten exclamation points, a colon, and a semicolon). As the final verse of the poem suggests (tongue-in-cheek), Corbière doesn't know "Art." But the "Art" to which he is referring is the classical seven-stringed lyre, the Euterpe-inspired lyricism of tradition. He *does*, however, know *an* art, namely, the poetry that he has created in "Ça?" and in the other texts of *Les Amours jaunes*, which sing, albeit in a cracked and off-key voice, to a clearly different drummer.

Because of the informal tone and disregard for rhetorical "accuracy" in Corbière's text, the problems of translation in "Ça?" are not concerned with some of the syntactic or lexical niceties that, let us say, characterize some of Mallarmé's or Valéry's poems. It is possible, therefore, to sacrifice precise meanings from time to time—and even to find colloquialisms in English corresponding to the "spoken" tone of the French—in favor of preserving the tone and oral flavor of the original. This explains the use, for instance, of expressions such as "guy" (v. 22) and "who knows" (v. 26), as well as that of ellipsis, contractions, and various expletives in my version. The first stanza of "Ça?" reveals a pair of puns that I have attempted to retain in English. In the opening verse, the French "essais"/"essayé" represents a pun based on the ambiguity between the literary form and the verb "to attempt" (to write). "Essayed" may be too learned in English, whereas "tried" still retains the pun (since "Essays" connote, besides their primary literal meaning, literary "tries"). In v. 3, the French "broché" may mean both "paper-bound" and "edited carelessly" (as opposed to "relié," either stylishly bound or "attached" to a traditional literary form): my "pasted" (a shortened form of "pasted together": the ellipsis of the latter word maintains the verse's appropriate tetrametrical rhythm), likewise, suggests both thoughtless editing (writing) and a flimsy (pasted) binding, thus (with "bound") retaining the tautology of the French ("broché"/"relié"). "Hocked" (v. 5) is the choice for "lavé" (cf. definition number ten in *Littré*). In the same verse, I have chosen "reed" over the more obvious—and literal—"lyre." First, the homophonic play on words in the French ("lyre"/"lire") must be preserved, as must, ideally, a parallel orthographic change ("lyre"/"lire"; "reed"/"read"). Further, the choice of "reed" retains the poetic or *lyr*ical (thus, musical) connotations of "lyre," since "reed" suggests very clearly the instrument of that archetypal musician, Pan. (The very same motif of music/poetry is expressed through the Pan or Faun figure, of course, by Mallarmé in his "L'Après-midi d'un faune.") In the same stanza, "wind-blown" is the choice for "décousu": as in the French expression, both the literal ("unsewn" or unattached) and figurative ("incoherent") meanings are thus allowed to coexist and to contrast with the adjective ending the previous verse. The fourth stanza presents several knotty problems. The verb *courir* appears three times, in each instance with a different connotative value: "pursue," "run," and "chase after" or "proposition." The puns result from the use of the same verb to describe the poet's pursuing "Originality"; the latter (or poetic inspiration) running away; and, finally, the figurative Originality-as-prostitute escaping the lascivious advances of these inspired poets. In English, one single word (e.g., "run") simply cannot convey this word play; consequently, I have chosen the word "pursue" twice, to establish a play for the third usage, in v. 16. First, "pursue" gives the second (off-)rhyme (with "neighborhood") to the stanza. More important, it allows the expression "flees with her purse" to enter into the joviality: a *cheville*, to be sure, but not altogether so, since it identifies Originality as a woman (of the streets) and adds "purse" to the two "pursues" in the quatrain, creating a pun perhaps somewhat forced, but corresponding nonetheless as nearly as possible to Corbière's. The stanza's third verse also presents a problem, since in the French, the expression "drôlesse assez drôle" represents yet another play on words, this time between the colloquial word for "tart" and the normal one for "funny" or "bizarre." (Corbière is still—ironically—referring to poetic Originality.) In English, the problem is to retain both the semantic content and the word play ("drôlesse"/"drôle"). Of the many words for "tart"—among which are "hussy," "harlot," "trollop," "jade," "strumpet," "wench," "jay," "tart" itself, and even "hooker"—and those for "funny" (e.g., "bizarre," "funny," "strange," "weird"), I first considered "hooker quite kooky," using the play of assonance as the basis for the pun. My final solution—based on both a semantic *and* phonetic equivalence in English—was "trull rather droll," which, although the substantive is somewhat esoteric, does retain enough phonemic similarity (between substantive and adjective) to create the desired parallel play on words. The word games continue in the following stanza. In a continuing (abortive) effort to identify the type of poetry he "writes," Corbière continues on his jolly way, this time (v. 18) using "haut" (as a sort of prefix) in another pun: "haut vol" ("high flight") and "haut-mal" (hyphenated, to mean "epilepsy"). My "high flight"/"high-fit" both identifies the latter as a physical anomaly (Corbière quite often refers to his verse as pathologically aberrant) and creates *phonetic* word play between "flight" and "fit." (The play in the French was based on the different *semantic* uses of "haut.") I have also chosen the off-rhyming pair "rasping"/"wings" to replace a similar sound play in the original consonant pair ("râle"/"d'ailes"). In the final two verses of the stanza, the *door* (to which Corbière's verse is escorted) becomes, playfully, an entire *house*: in fact, two of them, one of "ill repute" ("tolérance") and one of "detention" ("correction"). I have selected "That's close!" (more ornate than the French "Mais non!") to preserve the sound play from this stanza to the next ("Non"/"Bon" becomes "close"/"So"). In the opening verse of the sixth stanza the literal translation of "français" makes the rhyme extremely difficult: the substitution of "native," however (communicating the same semantic value as "French"), offers the desired assonant-rhyme with "made it." Finally, in the last stanza, "hit or miss" is inverted (without loss of meaning: in fact, the inversion adds a playful touch altogether consistent with the tone of the entire poem) to rhyme with the neutered "it" that represents the

"Art" Corbière insists is unknown to him, but that the careful reader will recognize as simply false modesty.

Epitaphe

A similar self-denigrating posing, as well as the same light, ironic tone and disrespect for acceptable poetic diction and rhetoric, occur in this *ante factum* epitaph. For sixty verses, Tristan paints himself as jack-of-all-trades-master-of-none: he possesses, alternately, "gold," "nerves," "verve," "soul," and "love"; he is an "ideal-seeker," uses "rich rhyme," and is considered to be a "poet," "artist," and "philosopher." But, as in "Ça?", every time he states a positive attribute of his own character at the beginning of a verse, he immediately undercuts it. But "Epitaphe" is more than a simple litany of contradictions: if it were this alone, why does Corbière carry on for so long, ostensibly repeating the same basic dilemma? The answer, surely, is that this is a poem, an "anesthetic" construct with its own integrity, its own complexities. And here lies (the pun, in this Corbiérian context, is appropriate...) *the* fundamental paradox of Corbière: the poet informs us (vv. 19-20) that he is a "Poète, en dépit de ses vers; / Artiste sans art,—à l'envers"; the only way in which this can be a poem and Corbière a poet is, then, if poetry can be written without *verses* and an artist can perform without *art*. But if we interpret these two terms in their broadest sense—that is, as the accepted esthetic norm of mid-nineteenth-century France—we then realize the significance of v. 29, "Ses vers faux furent ses seuls vrais." Corbière's intention is to write "false" (non-)verses, his only "real" ones. Accordingly, "Epitaphe" is replete with barbarisms: inconsistencies of versification, irregular stanzaic length, proliferating punctuation, conversational tone, use of puns and double-entendres, and so on.

The basic problems in translation presented by this text are similar to those encountered in "Ça?". In the second verse, "oversight" is chosen for "oubli," as the French expression "par oubli" suggests (as does the English expression) not only Tristan's oversight (i.e., his very life), but ours as well (i.e., we have all but forgotten him in the context of literary history). In v. 8, I have not retained *"je-ne-sais-quoi"* in its French form, although it is an accepted Gallicism in our language. The *"I-don't-know-what"* (although not as recognizable a locution) preserves the word play of the negative/verb *savoir*/complement sequence, the basis of the French play resulting from the reply to a *rhetorical* expression. In contrast, I have indeed retained the French (*"Rime riche"*) of v. 16, since "rich rhyme" is not properly English. In v.

20, "Artiste sans art" is translated as "Artist without art" (and not "Artless artist") for a specific reason: not only does it retain the ambiguity of the "sans art" (ingenuousness and absence of esthetics), but it better suggests an additional word play surely intended by Corbière in the original. "Artiste sans art" produces, if "sans" is taken in its most literal, mathematical sense (i.e., "Artiste" *minus* "art"), the suffix "-iste" (in English, "-ist"), or a "doer" or "maker" or "performer." Tristan is, however (according to his self-ironic perception), a nonspecialist, good at nothing (hence, "à l'envers"). In the following verse, the monorhymed tercet must be preserved, as well as the sense of "randomness" of the original "à tort à travers," difficult to translate. My "without rhyme or worse" performs this dual function, as well as adding two elements that corroborate the thematic thrust of the poem: "without rhyme" echoes "without art" and also ambiguously suggests that there is neither poetic rhyme nor *sense* ("rhyme") in Corbière's verse; and "or worse" implies that there is (purposely, again from Corbière's ironic viewpoint) no *reason* in this poetry, since "worse" is the very substitution for the expected "reason." ("Rhyme or reason" is, of course, a fixed English expression.) In v. 26, Corbière inserts the pun on the word "tête" (both "mug" and "mind"); a translation such as "What a mug!—but nothing upstairs" might suffice for the *meaning* but would, of course, neglect the desired pun of the original. My "A mind!—but never mind," while bypassing the physical/intellectual dichotomy, preserves the more essential (in the French) lexical word play (here, "mind"/"mind"). Two verses later, the French is again retained, at the risk of a tenuous rhyme ("*très*"/ "true"). I have rejected my original choice—"*quite*/His false verses were the only true ones he'd write"— because "*quite*" (although producing a "true" rhyme) does not (as does "*très*") preserve the pun based on the homophonic pair "trait"/"*très*." "*Lass*" (v. 31) was chosen over "maid," "girl," or "gal" for the rhyme with "second class" ("pacotille"). The same procedure applies to the choice of "good-for-nil," a colloquial rendering for the usual "good-for-nothing." (The following verse, as a result, had to be inverted, without loss of the semantic content.) Verse 37 presents, I think, an insuperable problem: there is not only the word play on "plat"/"plat" ("flat"/"plate") to consider, but also the expression "mettre les deux pieds dans le plat," in which "plate" is the French equivalent of the English "mouth." My version omits the original pun (on "plat"), but it does retain the rhyme by substituting the metonynic "bite" for the expected "mouth": admittedly, small consolation. In v. 47, the antithetical "goût" and "dégoût"—describing the antisocial, antiesthetic Tristan—are rendered as "gusto" and "disgusting," thus both preserving the phonetic word play and bringing attention to the literal, etymological meaning of the prefixed latter term. "Cuit" (v. 48) is also problematical, as it may mean both "cooked" (to contrast with the "cru" that precedes it) and "drunk." (Thus, "cru" may also mean both "raw" or "crude.") My "fried" retains this ambiguity, since it may mean either "cooked" or, in its colloquial sense, "stewed" or "crocked." In the penultimate verse of the poem, I have translated "mal planté" as "ill set": just as "mal planté" (as opposite of "bien planté") may imply both social standing and subterranean positioning (i.e., even Tristan's funeral was—will have been—botched), "ill set" (as opposite of "well set") produces the same word play, while contributing to a consonant-rhyme that concludes the poem.

I Sonnet

This little, apparently unassuming poem is typical of Corbière's perversity and constant deception of the reader. It is a "How To" poem, but in reverse. Taken literally (an egregious mistake for the reader!), "I Sonnet" is a rather obvious *ars impoetica*, a poem about how *not* to write poetry. The specific target of Tristan's attack is the precise, mechanical, formally exact manner of writing of the "Parnassian" poets of the 1860s and 1870s; ostensibly, the elements of parody—including allusions to classical mythology, sleep, mechanical paraphernalia, the title's Roman numeral, the peremptory subtitle, and the epigraph directed to hypothetical schoolmarms (or, ironically, to "budding young poets")—are quite accessible to the reader. But Corbière is a much more subtle poet than this: on a second level, he is also writing an *ars poetica*—not, as is traditional, by theory, but by actual practice—of his *own* unorthodox manner of writing. Seemingly spontaneous, the very personal techniques in evidence—which include puns, linked verbal associations (we notice subtle word networks concerning military discipline, sleep, mathematics, wires, and mythology, all of which poke fun at the classical, stiff, "soporific" Parnassian style), double-entendres, the use of actual numerals (unheard of until Tristan came along), and aberrant, nearly cancerous punctuation—create a subtle poem the execution of which reveals more than a modicum of care, control, and imagination.

The problems—of the original poem and the translation—in the initial quatrain all occur in the first two verses. The very first word, "Vers," may be rendered as "Verses" or "Lines": because these are quickly (and ironically) transformed into mechanical and *linear* entities—threads, soldiers, telegraph wires, and telegram lines—I have chosen the latter, which is appropriately ambiguous. The pun of "main"/"pied" ("hand"/"foot") is no problem, but "filés" is. It is perversely ambiguous: literally "spun," it also connotes wires ("fils"), which, indeed, reappear in vv. 6 and 8. Although the translation as "hand-spun" may suggest Clotho, the Greek Fate who spun the thread of life (and is thus appropriate to the ironic context of mythological allusion seen elsewhere in the poem), the expression "hand-wired" not only emphasizes the important element of mechanical and linear verse-fabrication, but it also implies that the poems under attack are, suspiciously, "home-made jobs." The first English equivalent of "uniforme" that comes to mind is "equal"; but "uniform" (*seemingly* a stiff literal rendering) is in fact a more effective choice, since it expresses both the literal "equal" while producing a pun—this was certainly Corbière's intention—on a *military* uniform. (Other allusions to the military reappear in vv. 2, 4, 13, and 14.) "Emboîtant bien le pas" (v. 2) means "falling nicely into step," but again Corbière is playing word games. Because "emboîtant" suggests "emboîtement" ("putting into boxes")—a perfect characterization of the stiff, incarcerating Parnassian style—I have chosen "box-step," which captures both these meanings and is the "dance analogue" of this poetic phenomenon of containment and absence of imagination. A knottier problem, however, is the French "peloton," which may mean both a ball of thread (theme of measurement, quantity) and a platoon of soldiers (theme of military—and poetic—discipline). "Bunch" was the closest I could come to expressing this ambiguity; as compensation, "bunch" produces a rhyme with "lunch." ("Go out to lunch" was the colloquial substitute in v. 3 for "fall asleep.") "En long" (v. 6) denotes "lengthwise" but also connotes "slumber" (elsewhere a motif, in vv. 3, 4, and 7), as in the expression "avoir les côtes en long," literally, "to have one's ribs lengthwise": thus, the choice of "sprawled out." "Pieu" (v. 7) poses another interesting problem in both the proper reading of the original text and in the options of translation. Literally, it means "post" or "stake." (It is, in context, a figurative expression of the poetic demarcation at the end of each verse represented by the rhyme.) In the context of the poem, however, there is a second possibility; "pieu" can also mean "bed" (a Picard form of the word "peau"—"skin"—on which one slept), appropriate to the "slumber" motif that obliquely pokes fun at the soporific Parnassian verse. The word that most closely incorporates both post and bed is "berth": in regard to the former, it cannot mean "post," but it *can* suggest distance (implicit in the post's—the rhyme's—demarcating function), as in the expression "to give wide berth to." "Give me some clues" (v. 9) is, admittedly, a free rendering of "à mon aide" ("help!"); but since the original locution is not in the least suggestive or ambiguous, this approximation—allowing for a rhyme with "Muse"—may be pardoned. The same is true for "wingèd steed," a periphrasis for Pegasus, where rhyme may supersede accuracy as a criterion for word choice. My neologism "delyrium" was chosen to suggest, like the French "délire" (although the French word has a *third* meaning not possible in English: "dé/lire" implies the undermining, by Corbière, of the normal *reading* process), both the denotative "delirium" and, since the word follows "lyre," the connotative and playful "de-lyre," or the pathological Parnassian avoidance of a Romantic overflowing beyond the prescribed boundaries of the poem. I have substituted a *y* for the expected *i* to compensate for the loss of a homonym in English ("lyre" has a long vowel sound; "delirium" does not), where it exists in the French ("lyre"/"lire"). Finally, I have selected "Attention" as the sonnet's last word instead of the more common English equivalent of the French "Attention," "Watch out." The advantage of this choice is that it may also be interpreted as the military command and may well have been meant as such by the poet, based on the other military allusions in the poem. (The precedent for using English in the sonnet has already been established by the *railway* of v. 5; this usage will reappear, for example, in Corbière's "A une demoiselle.")

BONNE FORTUNE ET FORTUNE

This is one of Tristan's frequent "antilove" poems: here, as elsewhere in his poetry, Corbière is the luckless dupe of Woman, portrayed in her usual role as street-walker. Interestingly, the same role is played by the poet's Muse, so that the act of devaluing remains essential, whether it pertains to love-making or verse-making. The first quatrain is entirely classical, complete with *rimes croisées*, caesuras where they should be (6/6), and—surprise!—a fourth verse as symmetrical as any written by Racine. But when the drama begins, that is, the confrontation between the female "ill-reputed" passerby and Tristan's internal hesitations, the proliferation of punctuation destroys what was originally a calm atmosphere and leads the reader to a typically ironic ending, in which the lady in question gives the unlucky poet a charitable donation (instead of the other way around), rather than the anticipated physical contact. The tone is, again, conversational and "nonliterary."

The problems of translation are less prominent here than in other, more complex texts. In the opening verse, "je fais mon trottoir," denoting "I go walking," may also connote street-walking, in the context of prostitution. The roles are thus reversed, as the love- (sex-) starved poet is the one patrolling the streets, as opposed to the prostitute, in French, the "fille de *trottoir*": "walk the streets," rather than the denotative "walk," preserves this ambiguity. "Part" (v. 2) is the equivalent of the French "air": I have chosen it over "air" or "look" for the rhyme with "heart" (v. 4). The inversion of the third verse in my version results from the same reason (the consonant-rhyme with v. 1), as does that of the sixth verse. In v. 7, "quel métier" is rendered "what a trade," not "what a life" or "what a job": indeed, Tristan is "trading" functions with the street-walking "passante." The pronoun at the end of v. 10 is converted into "that Doll." Even though this substantive does not appear in the French text, the colloquial "Doll" serves to specify the social status of the lady in question, as well as creating a rhyme with the "parasol" of the preceding verse. The "pennies" in the final verse, a rough equivalent of the French "sous" (they "carry over" the same idea of a paltry sum), creates an off-rhyme with "funny" of v. 11.

A UNE CAMARADE

The "pal" of this title (we should note that the poem is not dedicated to a "lover") is another "loose" woman, and the poem is an example (even more than "Bonne fortune et fortune") of the ironic presentation of Corbière as pitiful (non-)lover. In the opening stanza, Tristan is again playing games, not only with his heart, but with his words, as attested to by the pun "femme"/"fille" ("woman"/"wench") and the cacophonic fourth verse. In stanzas 2 and 4, the typical ironic undercut is employed: first, after comparing himself to a lizard and his "love" to a ray of light, Corbière finds Love a hindrance to this "sunbathing" (thus, logically, his "love" is "love-less"); and next, if his love is a "rare" bauble, it lacks the bauble's ability to be glued back together again. An incredible innocence—another pose—marks the sixth stanza, in which the poet attempts to avoid the blame for his amorous inactivity, as if the sexual act were some kind of fight. After terming his relationship, at best, "amitié calmée" and his friend a "mal-aimée" (Apollinaire may well have borrowed the term from this text for his celebrated "Chanson"), Tristan concludes the poem with a stanza that perverts everything: after love-making, cigarettes are typically smoked; here, where love is *not* made, a truce is the couple's only "token." If they die, it will not be from love, but from laughter. (The laughter of the "pal" in the final verse is surely sardonic, as is the "yellow"—jaundiced—laughter of Mount Etna: see, below, the discussion of "A l'Etna.")

In the opening verse, the play on "fille" (which suggests both the feminine gender of the "girl" and the pejorative sense of "wench") and "femme" may be preserved by the choice of "bitch": other expressions fail, as they must make a choice between one connotation or the other. In the following verse, "nice child" is the more literal possibility; but "good Joe," besides affording a rhyme, is consistent with the colloquial tone (it is comparable to "good guy") and, perhaps more important, by its masculinity ("Joe") neutralizes the femininity of the "pal" (altogether consistent with her role in the poem—see the title and vv. 23 and 30—and indeed in Corbière's poetry in general). The order of imperatives in v. 3 is changed, without loss of meaning, to provide the rhyme with v. 1. In v. 12, I have used a (the pun is again appropriate) "free" translation of "liberté," which I have converted into an adjective and to which I have added the proverbial "as a bird." This "liberty" may, as I have mentioned, be taken with the oral, colloquial texts of Corbière, if the context (as here) warrants it. (A major motive here was, of course, the rhyme with v. 10.) Other examples of "padding with impunity" occur in vv. 13 and 27, where, this time for rhythmic purposes (to preserve the tetrameter), I have added "perhaps" and "maybe," respectively. I have retained, in vv. 15-16, the word play on "se recolle"/"décollé" by using the pair "glued"/"unglued": the latter is placed—out of order, but at no loss—at the end of the verse, for the assonant-rhyme with "suit" of v. 14. In the fifth stanza, the slippery "rendu" may be rendered (the temptation to pun *chez* Corbière is often overpowering...) as "beat," which may mean either "tired" ("fatigué") or "beaten" (into the ground), both of which aptly describe the "paradise" to which the poet is alluding. In the next verse, the "greenness" of the apple (of original sin) refers primarily to the motif of innocence (which the poet prefers, ironically, to sexual contact). But besides meaning "green" or "innocent" or "unripe," it may also mean "sour": I have chosen this latter expression, since it not only provides a consonant-rhyme with "door," but it also appropriately suggests the avoidance of the sweetness of a sexual encounter with the "pal" of the title. In v. 23 (and, subsequently, v. 24), I have selected "Which one" and not "Who" for the pronoun "Quel." What this does is, again (as in the French), to depersonalize the "couple," as do the masculine references to the female persona. Likewise, in the second part of this same verse, "bon apôtre," a colloquial euphemism (with a blatantly masculine substantive), is rendered as the equally colloquial and virilizing "brother." The pun in v. 28 presents another problem in translation. Corbière uses the verb *tromper* in its two principal senses: "to cheat on" (deceive or betray, in the sexual sense) and "to be cheated" (misled or disappointed). The verb "cheat," therefore, must be used twice in the verse to retain the pun. The "chère mal-aimée" (v. 31) is a neologism, employed by Corbière to contrast with the expected, intimate "chère bien-aimée," the "dearly belovèd" of nuptial (and pre-nuptial) parlance. My "dearly mislovèd" is, in the interests of fidelity, also a neologism, and the *grave* accent is retained not only for the rhyme, but as an ironic parallel (as Tristan himself intended) to the expected "belovèd." The penultimate verse is inverted, both for the rhyme ("gall"/"all") and to avoid the placement of "laughter" twice as end-rhyme.

A UNE DEMOISELLE

Corbière is not a particularly difficult poet (at least compared to Mallarmé, for instance), in terms of "understanding" the basic language of his verse. Rather, his innovation and imagination are based on subtle and ingenious word play that is easily lost or unappreciated if his poems are read hastily or "just for their meaning." This sonnet is, nonetheless, one of his more "difficult pieces" (cf. v. 7), more difficult to read and to translate than most of his other offerings: the English version attempts to reflect the characteristic word play and subtle puns. "A une demoiselle" is quite similar to "I Sonnet" in regard to the indirect manner by which it posits its own esthetics; whereas the latter poem does this at the expense of a poetic technique it attacks, the esthetic target of this poem is a false way of emoting and of self-expression. Why esthetic? Because the damsel who is criticized is described metaphorically as a piano, and because the means of expression contrasted with this artificial one (her "playing" is monotonous and artificial) is in fact Corbière's own poetry ("cet accord de ma lyre," v. 9). The techniques used in the poem, substitutes for the artificial piano-playing (the emoting of the lady), are all spontaneous, discordant, and (for Corbière) natural (thus, antitraditional): proliferating punctuation, puns, neologism, ellipsis, and the chaotic rhythm of the tercets.

The lady's piano with its artificial notes is an Erard, a traditional and popular French make. An equivalent transposition should be made (since few English readers would recognize the French company), but which of the "big two" should be chosen—Steinway or Baldwin? They are both "middle-class" instruments, but Baldwin seemed a more universal choice, in addition to which is the bonus of the name itself: "bald" suggests its antidote, "wig," which is artificial, and thus appropriate to the appositional phrase, "râtelier osanore." "Osanore" (artificial teeth: a rare word) produces a redundancy, since "râtelier" already means dentures. (The "teeth" of the piano are false: the "saws" of v. 2 suggests monotony, as "dent" may mean either human tooth or saw's tooth.) My choice of "inauthentic" (and not "falsified" or "artificial") is perhaps more subtle than the original word, but its advantage is to retain the original etymological significance. That is, "osanore" is made up of three words—"os" (bone), "an" (Greek for "without"), and "or" (gold). It means, literally, a "goldless tooth," an artificial one without value, made of hippopotamus ivory. "Inauthentic" has embedded in it *au*, the Latin symbol for gold. "Click-clack" ("monotonous") is also the repetitive sound made by a mill and announces the metaphorical "miller's nightmare" of v. 5. Instead of the literal "sonorous clavier" (v. 3), I have used the equally (perhaps more...) ironic "musical adventure," which offers a rhyme with v. 1. The "strands" of v. 8 replaces one word play for another (while salvaging the rhyme): whereas the French "accents" *diacritically* echoes the "croches" of the same verse, the English "strands" *thematically* echoes the tonsorial "cheveux" of v. 4. The tercets, presenting numerous difficulties in reading, are no easier to translate. "Accord" can best be rendered as "harmony," to produce an ironic double-entendre: in its own way, Corbière's music is "harmonic," as opposed to the dull, feeling-less, "melodic" scratchings of the lady's instrument that must, literally, "decipher" these strange strains; further, "accord" may mean "harmony" in the sense of its cognate, "accord," suggesting that Corbière alone is attuned to his own music. The hyphenation in v. 10 attempts to capture the monotonous, functional, "ready-made" quality of the piano-playing. This punctuation is, I believe, the closest English equivalent to the fixed French usage, "*x* à *y*" (e.g., "pince à linge," "clothespin"), that is, something made *for the purpose of* performing a specific function. The harpsichord's "translation" is rendered as "become versifier," not only for the rhyme, but also to maintain the irony of doubting the piano's ever becoming anything approaching the "poetic." Excluding the final word, v. 11 describes the discordant noises that the Corbiérian "lyre" makes in the name of rebellion and unorthodoxy. "Cri d'os" (shriek of bones) is a strange alliance, but we may recognize, upon close reading, a Corbiérian pun: the English "credo." These noises are, after all, among the few things in which Corbière had any *belief*. This interpretation is not as far-fetched as one might imagine, however, since puns on English words are not uncommon in his poetry; and even in this poem, we have an "English" pun in v. 12, to be discussed shortly. At any rate, there is seemingly no way to retain this play on words in English, unless the choice is "bone-crush." Now "crush" does differ, semantically and admittedly, from "shriek." But, first, it does suggest destruction, as does "shriek," which destroys the harmony classical music was intended to produce. Second, the [k] sound (with the two that follow) reproduces the same harsh sound of the French verse. Third, and most important, the English "credo" is now reversed—in an English translation, it is now the *French* word that appears within the English—and "crush" (if pronounced ever-so-improperly) produces the agrammatical "crois-je" ("I *do* believe"). "Stri*k*es and cra*c*ks" (as the cracking of the voice, the harmony of Corbière's lyre is perceived by ordinary musicians as imperfect) replaces the harsh sounds of the French "pl*aque* et *ca*sse" with its own. In the same verse, we find the neologism "Plangorer," from the Latin *plangere*, "to bemoan." My own neologism is thus in order, and I have selected "Plangorify" over the more logical "Plangorate" for the rhyme. The puns now begin to accumulate and to destroy the classical harmony of "normal" poetic language. Rejecting the "moaning" route, Corbière now rejects the presence of classical music (the lady's piano) as the proper agent for the expression of real feelings. In v. 12, "Sol" (G: a recognized, traditional note), says Tristan, isn't the way to express one's inner feelings. The key here is to recognize the pun on "Sol," not only a musical key, but also the near-homonym of the English word... "soul" ("âme"). In my version, there is again a trade-off (in the form of a transfer of the actual words on which the pun is based): the pun is now between the French "clef" (of "Treble-clef") and the English translation, "key." The following verse contains another word game: this time, *"Fa"* is both the *F* note and the initial sound of *"Fe*mme" ("Woman"). In the English version, "Femme" is translated as "Effeminacy" (and not "Woman"), since *"Ef*feminacy" has as *its* first sound... *F*. Finally, the pun in v. 14 of the original is based on the double meaning of "soupir": "rest" (in music, a "demi-soupir" is an eighth-rest) and "sigh" (from the verb *soupirer*). The English incorporates the pun based on "eighth-*rests*... *repose*." "Repose," not present in the original, had to be included to create this word play, but it is not inappropriate when juxtaposed with the affective and leisurely "sigh" that appears at the poem's conclusion.

RAPSODIE DU SOURD

This poem is among Corbière's most profound metaphorical statements of his separation—physical, esthetic, sexual, and social—from the rest of humanity. (In "Le Poète contumace," he aptly describes himself, through the poet-persona, as "en dehors de l'humaine piste.") Metaphorical, because what is in question is not Tristan's suspected deafness as biographical fact (impossible to prove, despite various abortive attempts), but his isolation from human intercourse stemming from a figurative "amputation" of his hearing. The operation to remove his hearing in the poem is all the more poignant, since Corbière did indeed consider his physical impairments (rheumatism, tuberculosis, an imagined ugliness, etc.) as the source of much of his unhappiness, and because the malefactor, in this instance, is a doctor, a "man of art" (and, judging from "Ça?" and "Epitaphe," we know what he thinks of the latter) who represents a person of "correct" social stature. The poem is basically a series of "ravings" by the poet, cut off from others by his inability to hear, doubting his own humanity and his powers of communication by means of conventional language. At the conclusion, the poet asks his female companion (his "contemplative Idol") to join him in silence, the only possible remaining method of communication. But we should by now be wise enough to Tristan's poetic posing to sense that the operation is simply a tongue-in-cheek ploy to divert the reader's attention away from a more subtle proposition: if the deaf-man (the poet-persona) is incoherent, "muzzled," and, eventually, mute (Tristan's human situation), Corbière, as always, has full control of his text (his poetic situation), creating his inimitable brand of antilyricism, based on sound play (particularly significant in this context of deafness), word play, and assorted aberrations from the traditional mould.

The rhyme pattern is especially unpredictable (not for Corbière, but in contrast to the expected consistency in a lyrical text), switching from *rimes plates* to *rimes croisées* without notice or apparent reason. (The poet's loss of hearing may have something to do with this!) I have preserved this pattern in my version. Blatant (and conscious) *enjambements* have also been retained, in vv. 2-3, 5-6, 9-10, 40-41, 43-44, and 45-46. In one instance (vv. 14-15), I have inserted one not present in the original, for purposes of rhyme ("greet"/"meet"). I have also retained the only two octosyllabic verses in the poem (6, 8). The choice of "taking in" (v. 4) was made in order to preserve a double-entendre: the French verb *entendre* (as in "double-entendre"!) may mean both "to hear" and "to understand." Because Corbière doubtless intended the verb to suggest ironically both senses, my verb thus functions in the same way. In the following verse, "thanks a bunch" takes liberties with the simple "merci" in the French, but the colloquial irony is justified here by the ironic "vous qui daignez" that follows. The conscious reverberation of sounds in vv. 8-9 ("orgueil"/"œil") is reflected by the assonance of my "pride"/"eye." In v. 10, "au clou" may refer both to the "deaf" ear and back to the "cercueil" of v. 6 (i.e., the poet's head is a figurative coffin, the ear the aperture through which a nail is driven). My "nailed up" suggests the same ambiguity of physical and figurative deafness/death. The sound play of vv. 11-12 ("face"/"face"/"bassement") is preserved by the retaining of "face" twice in the English (although the more literal "opposite me" might have been chosen in the second instance) and the addition of a third long *a* sound in "basely." In the same verse (12), "drool insults" is faithful to the original ambiguous expression, "baver," which may mean both "drool" *and* "insult." In vv. 13-14, "Demain" and "Dans la rue" are inverted in my version, for the purpose of rhyme. "En radouci" is rendered as *sotto / Voce*. Although there is no Italian in the original poem, the expression has been sufficiently assimilated into our language to allow this equivalent: the rhyme is again the motivating factor. The "corne" of v. 17 is significant in the poem's context, as it initiates a network of musical expressions consciously inserted by Corbière for ironic purposes. (The others are "guitare," "trompe," "cor," "clarinette," and "tam-tam.") My "trumpets" both retains this musical motif and, semantically, expresses the volume with which others must speak to the now-deaf poet. The expression "*trompe-d'Eustache*" (v. 29) represents a typical pun: "trompe" is, anatomically, a (Eustachian) tube; but its other meaning ("trump" or "horn") obtains as well, as part of the musical motif just noted. (In fact, the "cor" at the end of this same verse confirms the pun.) I have attempted to preserve the pun by my "*Eustachian tuba*." The next problem this poem presents to the translator—namely, the opening verse of the ninth stanza—is nearly insurmountable (and, for that very reason, a fascinating one). The verse represents a wonderful use of cacophony, perhaps unequalled in nineteenth-century French verse, with the possible exception of Mallarmé's celebrated "Aboli bibelot d'inanité sonore" (in "*Ses purs ongles très haut dédiant leur onyx…*"). A literal translation most nearly preserves the sounds of the French, but what to do with "Tantalus" as an end-rhyme? I have settled, begrudgingly, with "up" as an assonant-rhyme with the short *u* of the Greek personage. The other problem is that the French verse is framed (purposely) by the same sound ([ik]), which in English is all but lost, except for the identical *al* sound of "Hysteric*al*"/"Tant*al*us." In the eleventh stanza, "Rien" demands a monosyllabic analogue in English, for the rhythm of the tetrameter. As "Nought" is too learned for this context (as contrasted with the opening verse of Mallarmé's "Salut," discussed below), "Zilch" is the colloquial, but not inappropriate, solution. In the final verse of the stanza, "bouché" suggests both the closed note of the clarinet and, in familiar usage, "stupid": my "closed-minded" also suggests both meanings. "Soûl" (v. 47) is, literally, "drunk"; my "smashed" conveys this meaning in its colloquial form, while also communicating the broken springs of the balance-wheel that, in the deaf poet's head, has gone haywire. In the next-to-last stanza, "sourde" may mean both "deaf" and "dark" (the pun is based on the expression, "lanterne sourde," "dark lantern"); I have used both adjectives, as a single one connoting both possible meanings was beyond the realm of availability. In the next verse, "vibrait" is rendered as "was moving," since this particular expression (and not the more literal "vibrate") also preserves the *affective* connotation of *vibrer* ("le cœur"), as intimated by the "cœur" of the stanza's opening verse.

A L'ETNA

It was as if all the flowers with which Corbière had ever played that "She loves me / She loves me not" game had even-numbered petals! His complete failure to develop a heterosexual relationship was probably the most painful aspect of his exile from the rest of humanity and an important preoccupation of his verse. Sickly from his youth to his death (he died at the age of twenty-nine, following continuous bouts with chronic rheumatism and tuberculosis), and not endowed with attractive features (his exaggerated conception of himself as a repulsive beast never wavered, confirmed by his frequent author's signature—"une gueule," "a mug"—under his drawings and caricatures), he had early on developed an ironic conception of love. The title of his only collection of verse—*Les Amours jaunes*, or *Jaundiced Loves*—is significant. "A l'Etna" is one of numerous illustrations of this theme. (We have already seen it in "Bonne fortune et fortune" and "A une camarade.") Since a normal heterosexual relationship was impossible, Corbière often substituted some (usually non-human) entity for his true identity. In one poem ("Sonnet à Sir Bob"), the lady is a prostitute, and the poet wishes to be her dog in order to receive her affection. Here, Mount Etna is the surrogate female and as such can be approached by the poet with impunity (i.e., without fear of rejection). The "plot" is simple: the poet makes advances toward the old, sickly, time-ravaged volcano, wishing to take her to bed (and inciting her jealousy by bragging of his conquest of her rival, Vesuvius), as they would indeed make an ideal couple. (Both are sickly and "more or less" old hands at making love.) The tone is unabashedly ironic, making fun of Tristan in particular, Woman in general, and the absurd world of love-making in toto.

In the first stanza, Corbière seems to be taunting Etna (as a come-on, to excite her jealousy) with the story of his conquest of Vesuvius. Superficially (thus, literally), the language is that of ascent and descent, in mountain terms: "monté" (he has climbed Vesuvius) and "baissé" (Vesuvius has declined in intensity). But the chosen words ("monté," "baissé") conceal some subtle word play: "monter" may also suggest sexual mounting, and "baisser" is a near-homonym of "baiser" (colloquially, "to have intercourse"). My renderings—"I've mounted Vesuvius," "Vesuvius has been humping less"—thus retain both the literal actions and the more colloquial, sexual connotations. Likewise, the "hotter" (for "warmer") in v. 3 preserves both the thermal and sexual implications of the word "chaud." I have, further, allowed "less" (v. 2) and "more" (v. 4) to appear together in the same stanza, to be echoed in the final verse of the poem. The comparison of volcano to woman—made in earnest by a bourgeois mentality—is mocked by Corbière in vv. 5-7; the volcano herself seems to share the poet's irony, in v. 8. "Bust a seam," instead of simply "burst," is a slight embellishment; but it does not distort the meaning and retains the *rime plate* of the original. Similarly, "Let's hit the sack" (v. 13) is a more colloquial version than the original "Couchons ensemble"; but it reflects the casualness of tone that was Corbière's intent. "Confrere" for "Comrade" ("Camarade") deserves a special explanation. The original "Camarade" implies a passionless, almost *fraternal* affair (cf. "A une camarade"): "Con*frere*" not only captures this shade of meaning, but it also announces the "frères" ("brothers") of v. 15. This is a somewhat rare example of an expression used in translation that justifiably contributes to the text some shade absent in the original. Here, "Confrère" in the French would be too obvious and heavy a repetition of the "frères" that appears two verses later. "Flank" for "side" (v. 14) suggests the intended dehumanization of the sexual relationship. I have inverted the order of both vv. 14 and 16, for purposes of rhyme: nothing is "lost in translation."

PAYSAGE MAUVAIS

This poem is placed in the *Armor* section of *Les Amours jaunes*, which deals with quite a different subject than the majority of Corbière's poems: not Tristan himself, but his native Brittany. Absent from this section is the now-familiar ironic tone, the self-deprecation, the poetic posing. The style of "Paysage mauvais" is also different from that of the poems in the first four sections of the *recueil*: it is far less self-conscious, much more conservative, and certainly lacks the exhibitionism of the preceding texts. It is a kind of "tone poem" that attempts to present the mood of Brittany with its Celtic mythology, its fantasy, and its sinister qualities. Its structure is also different, consisting of a series of nouns (with or without verbs), one following the other, which produces the effect of cumulative description rather than the suspense, antithesis, undercutting, etc., to which we have now been accustomed. This is the first poem we have seen so far in which the language does not overpower the subject matter. Here, what is engrossing is the fantastic countryside and its inhabitants: the sands, the marsh, the moon, the hare, the Laundress (in Celtic mythology, she washes the clothes of the dead), the toads (with the owl and the cuckoo, Celtic symbols of the sinister and death). The language is (for Corbière) rather traditional: there is, for instance, classical inversion (v. 10) and images that evoke (rather than call attention to themselves as linguistic entities)—metaphorical bone beaches, personified waves that cough the death-knell, the moon mysteriously swallowing worms, the cooking fever, the metaphorical hare-wizard, the wolves' sun (the moon), and the toad-stools. The images result, then, in the most expressive feature of the poem—the vibrancy, animation, and fantasy of the mysterious Breton landscape.

The adjective in the title is rendered as "dark," not "bad," since its inversion with the substantive changes its ordinary moral connotation to a more sinister, foreboding one. Sounds are, as in many other poems (cf. "Rapsodie du sourd"), essential to retain; but now the function is evocative, not ironic or playful. The *l*'s and *a*'s of the opening verse are transferred to *o*'s and *n*'s in my version. Likewise, the sound patterns of the third verse determine the choice of "wan," "swamp," and "chomps" (rather than, say, "pale," "marsh," or "swallows"): "—*Palud pâle, où la lune avale*" becomes "—*Wan swamp, where the moon chomps.*" "Rhoncus" is chosen over "rattles" or "coughs," both for the rhyme and for the rhythm of the second verse: to preserve the tetrameter, a monosyllable is needed before the colon, which necessitates the switch from substantive to verb for "Des glas." I have selected "chime" (v. 2) over the more literal "sound," again for the rhyme, and also to repeat the specific (figurative) bell-like sound made by the waves' rattle. "Giant," not "great" or "huge" (v. 4), seems to suggest better the fabulous nature of the worms eaten by the moon.

"Fries" was chosen over "bakes" for its sonorous qualities: it partici-
pates in a sequence of sounds—alliteration with "Fever" and assonance with "sprite"—closer to the original French alliterations
("Calme"/"Cuit," "fièvre"/"follet") and assonance ("Cuit"/"languit").
The relative pronoun construction was avoided in v. 8, as "in flight"
affords a rhyme with v. 6. In v. 12, I have sacrificed syntactic accuracy
for the only possible rhyme ("melancholic"/"colic," which, moreover,
reflects the parallel phonetic structure in the French), having to use
both an inversion not warranted by the French substantive-adjective
positioning and the slightly archaic form of the adjective. The play of
the final word of the poem is based on the metaphorical source of
"mushrooms," which is etymological: it comes from the Breton expression *skabellon tonsegad*. "Escabeau" is a stool (here, literally, a
"toad-stool," or the actual "residence" of the toad), and my "stool-
abodes" thus preserves the etymological pun (as well as, of course, the
rhyme with "toads").

PETIT MORT POUR RIRE

This delicate piece is part of the final section of *Les Amours jaunes*,
Rondels pour après, which has received only scant critical attention: an
unfortunate oversight, as they are among the loveliest songs written in
French and are "modern" precursors of many twentieth-century
texts. These *rondels*—totally different from anything else Corbière
ever wrote—are filled with lovely rhythms, strange and powerful imagery, and delicate sonorities. Their theme is the (posthumous) return to the world of childhood that is simple, marvelous, visionary. In
terms of form, the *rondels* are also extraordinary (in the context of
Corbière's *œuvre*) for their sectional unity: except for the opening
piece ("Sonnet posthume"), they are *rondels* that have been altered
from the classical form perfected in the fifteenth century by Charles
d'Orléans (thirteen verses, two rhymes, varying refrains); they are all
in italics; they are directed to the "enfant," a poet-persona different
from any of the other ones employed by Tristan; they are all in the
future tense, pointing to posthumous renewal; and they all contain
the same type of novel imagery. In "Petit mort pour rire," the phenomenon of death, especially tragic (normally) for one so young, is
transformed into an experience of liberation. The "enfant" is endowed with supernatural powers, and natural surroundings partici-
pate in the child's portrayal: grass becomes his hair, fire dances out of
his sockets, and flowers people his laugh. If this world is strange, it is
also misunderstood by the bourgeois masses of the real world. (This is

one of the recurrent motifs of many of the "poètes maudits.") For the bourgeois, death is final, and the coffin is simply a hollow box in which to place the man/fiddle who, in death, has ceased to play his tune. But they are wrong, since death is only the beginning of a wonderful renewal, for the child in these *rondels* and, perhaps, for Corbière himself, who, although an atheist of sorts, may well have believed—at the very end of his sorrowful existence—in some redemptive return to innocence, in a world after death in which what was (with the possible exception of the creative act itself) total failure in his "real" life might be eternally reversed.

The pun in the title is occasioned by Corbière's play on the expression "petit mot pour rire," a "little joke": here, death is a slight event, to be regarded without the usual solemnity. My title preserves this word play, while suggesting ironically that the early demise of the "enfant" would have been passed off with anticipated sentimentality by the bourgeois' "pauvres têtes." What is essential to preserve in this poem is, first, the difficult rhyme pattern of the *rondel* form (here, ABBA/ABA/ABBAA). Limiting the poem to only two rhymes must, of course, result in problems of word choice: in being faithful to the rhyme scheme, I have attempted to resolve them all, but in some cases (end of v. 8, for instance, to be discussed below), I have had to settle for less-than-ideal solutions. The "comber of comets" is not a surprising juxtaposition, even more successful in English, from an etymological point of view: "comet" comes from the Greek word "komé," meaning "hair." (By metonymy, the hair-like tail becomes the comet itself.) The same word choice occurs in Mallarmé's *"La chevelure vol d'une flamme..."* and Charles Cros' "Scherzo." In v. 4, "prisonniers" is rendered as "imprisoned lie," for the rhyme (without, however, loss of the basic meaning). "Amourettes" (v. 5) is, in my version, "Love's Sigh": an equivalent translation for the French-named flower, but "amourette" in French can also mean "love affair." Verses 6 and 7 are reversed, again to maintain the stanza's original rhyme scheme (ABA). I have substituted the hyperpoetic "forget-me-ne'er" for "forget-me-not," again for the rhyme. There is a pun embedded here that does *not* appear in the French (the poem is none the worse for it, however): "oubliette," meaning "dungeon," suggests *oublier*, "to forget." *Robert* gives as two definitions of "lourd": "stupid" or "maladroit" (intellect) and "heavy" (weight). Thus, "Don't play the heavy" (v. 8) suggests both that the "enfant" should avoid being "heavy," or a dead weight; and that indeed it is the *bourgeois* who play the "stupid" role in life. The "why" at the end of the verse is an unfortunate result of the attempt to retain the rhyme scheme; it *is* a *cheville*, yet (if one is to justify it at all...) it does reflect the lightly didactic tone. (The poet is giving advice to the child/poet.) A final compromise of the difficult rhyme pattern is "Another bourgeois lie," which, although not a literal translation (it reflects mendacity rather than the stupidity suggested in the above discussion of "lourd"), reveals nonetheless the mocking, disapproving attitude of the poet.

STÉPHANE MALLARMÉ

The opening piece of Mallarmé's collected poems, "Salut," is what it announces itself to be: a toast the poet made to a group of young poets at a banquet held by the journal *La Plume* in 1893. It is a strange toast, but typical of Mallarmé's manner of expression, in that it is elliptical, extremely suggestive, and terribly difficult both semantically and syntactically. If we *had* to paraphrase the poem—for the purposes of orientation and clarity—we might explain it in the following way: Mallarmé is looking at the bubbling foam in his champagne glass (he compares it to both "nothing" and "virgin verse") and imagines a group of sirens diving head-first into the bubbles. Continuing the maritime motif, he imagines himself on the poop of the "good ship poetry" (he was generally acknowledged as the dominant figure of French "Symbolism" and was the perennial host of the famous "Tuesday night" poetry gatherings in his apartment on the rue de Rome), with his younger protégés at the prow. He then proposes the actual toast (in the final tercet), dedicated to anything worthy of the painstaking and solitary act of writing poetry. Our mistake, of course, is to "reduce" the poem to such a description: that may be what the sonnet is superficially "about"; but the real—indeed, the *only*—subject of the poem is, as always with Mallarmé, the poem itself, its elusive language, its metaphorical signifying, the suggestiveness of its words. "Salut" is, quite literally, *about* "nothing," the concept of ultimate reduction to nothingness, the dialectic of poetic fertility and sterility, the "blank page" or the limits of painful condensation, which was Mallarmé's ideal, but never-realized creative gesture.

The very first word is essential, since it not only represents the entire focus of the poem but also presents a difficult problem in reading and translation. "Rien" is invariably translated elsewhere as either "Nothing" or some synonym such as "Nil" or "Nought." But in order to preserve the total impact of this expression as it was intended, we should first note that it (an *absence*) is, curiously, in apposition with two *presences*—"foam" and "verse." The implications are that: 1. both foam and verse are so evanescent and tenuous that they may disintegrate into nothingness (indeed, the self-destruction of a poem in front of our very eyes is a frequent strategy of the poet; here, the foam "designates only the cup," i.e., has no substance, but suggests, by metonymy, only its container); and 2. these "nothings"—as entities—are, paradoxically, the very essences of a Mallarmé poem. In this light, we must now appreciate the other, less common implications of our original problem-word, "Rien." It may indeed mean—when not accompanied by the negativizing "ne" that produces "nothing": *our* "rien," in this poem, is in fact thus unaccompanied—either "little" (a euphemism, as in "I got that for nothing") or—from its Latin source *rem*, accusative form of *res*, "thing"—"anything." (This is in fact confirmed by the three examples of poetic subject in v. 12, followed by the "whatever" that merits poetic concern.) "Nothing," then, will not suffice to incorporate all this: I have instead selected "Ought." Although it is slightly archaic in its negative usage, it does have the distinct advantage of the dual polar meanings needed here: it can mean, on the negative hand, "nothing" (synonymous with "nought" or "aught"); and, on the positive, it can be construed as a form of the verb "owe," which comes from the Anglo-Saxon verb *agan*, "to have or possess." (Etymology and its resultant word play, for Mallarmé as for Valéry, plays an essential role in the choice of words.) The connotations of the verbal "ought" (in addition to its supremely positive etymological source) are all on the positive side of nothing, whether they suggest obligation, desirability, or probability. And—significantly—a secondary positive meaning (as noun) is "anything" or *"whatever,"* which corresponds precisely to v. 13 ("To whatever..."), in apposition to "Rien." The next two verses present an equally thorny but intriguing problem. In the original poem, Mallarmé has subtly and purposely juxtaposed the two words "Telle" and "loin," a strange coupling indeed (an adverbialized adjective—syntactically displaced, no less—followed by an adverb). "Telle" (a typically Mallarméan expression, because of its nearly-superfluous status as adverb and cosmic, generalizing function as adjective) may at first seem gratuitous or even the wrong choice (it means "such," but here it is used adverbially to describe the action of the troop of sirens), but its appearance right next to "loin" cannot be accidental. Instead of using a more orthodox word to mean "thus" or "so" (e.g., "ainsi," "donc"), Mallarmé has chosen "Telle," which, if we eliminate one of the *l*'s, gives us the Greek word for "far off" (as in *"tele*phone," etc.). This is, of course, cleverly confirmed in the very next word ("loin"), suggesting that words, above all else, are the actual subject of the toast... and the poem. If Mallarmé can make nothing from something (words) in poems like the "sonnet en -yx" (which we shall discuss below), here he creates verbal association from an ostensibly gratuitous usage. Although my "Tell" is not the precise English meaning of "désigne," it does express the act of denotation or simple statement represented by the French verb and, more important, retains the etymological word play of the original juxtaposition of "Telle" and "loin." This strategy is, I feel, essential to the translation, although not without sacrifice: the resultant verses are either a bit too short (v. 2) or too long (v. 3), disturbing the quatrain's rhythmic equilibrium. The "myriad" of v. 4 was chosen for its *préciosité*: like "myriad," the French "mainte" is a formal, literary, and slightly archaic alternative to other expressions of quantity (e.g., "beaucoup de," "bien des," "nombreuses," etc.). More important, in the French, the adjective is intentionally displaced (it modifies the "troupe" of the previous verse, not the "sirènes" of the same one); "sirens many" might give the reader the mistaken impression that it modifies the substantive "sirens" and would thus undermine Mallarmé's intention of syntactic disorientation. "Inverse" (v. 4) was selected for the *rime riche* with v. 1: this seemed appropriate, since the original's are very *riches*, and many of the other rhymes I have had to settle with here (in order to preserve more essential elements) are only off-rhymes. I have rendered "fastueux" (v. 7) as "festive" (it is elsewhere translated as anything from "gorgeous" to "gaudy"), which incorporates the dual connotations of the celebration of the word that all true poets share and the celebration that was the generating source or "pre-text" of the poem (the banquet itself). "Tides," not "waves," next to "thunder," produces a quasi-alliteration close to the original "*f*lots de *f*oudre." "Sunders" ("coupe") and "thunders" was tempting as a rhyme, but I thought it better to retain the ABBA/ABBA rhyme of the original quatrains. In v. 9, "calm" follows "transport" because in the French, "belle" is placed uncharacteristically (but for emphasis) *after* its modified substantive. (I have tried throughout to be consistent in this reversal of adjective placement, since in French adjectives that usually precede their nouns are placed after—and vice versa—for stylistic reasons: this displacement often intensifies the adjective's— moral or affective—impact.) "Transport," not "drunkenness," because of its nautical connotation: this choice suggests both inebriation (at the banquet) and the rocking (of the slightly tipsy Mallarmé), which is that of man (literal) and boat (figurative), the latter confirmed by the "tangage" ("pitch") that qualifies "ivresse" in the very next verse. "Enlists" was not selected solely for the rhyme: the French "engage" may mean either "invites" or, in a military context, "enlists." (After all, Mallarmé and his fellow poets are now, within the image the poet has created, sailors.) "Propose," not "offer," creates, with "t*o*ast," an assonance, close to the French vowel sequence "deb*ou*t... sal*u*t." The final tercet presents some difficult problems. "Most" (v. 13) is not in the original poem; but the past definite "valut" ("deserved") suggests a superlative, a *val*orized, single-minded quest that only belongs to the "happy few," the chosen poets. It also, secondarily, supplies a convenient rhyme with "toast." I have selected "blank" over the literal "white" of the sail, which color is self-evident. Mallarmé's "whiteness" invariably intimates the vacant blankness of the paper, symbol of the poet's "concern," his tireless, perilous quest for the ideally condensed, hence absent (again: "Rien") poem. But the most difficult problem concerns the tercet's rhyming verses, 12 and 14. It all begins with "toile," which, in context, is purposely ambiguous: it may mean either "sail" (a synecdoche for the poetic "boat" that carries Mallarmé and his protégés) or, again synecdochically, the figurative "canvas" of the poet's art. If "sail" is chosen in the English version, there remains the problems of 1. rhyme ("star"/"sail"?: one solution would be to reverse the order of "reef" and "star" in v. 12, then to change "reef" to "shoal"—a consonant-rhyme with "sail"—since the sand of the shoal represents a sort of granular equivalent to the metaphorical danger for poets Mallarmé has in mind in the rocks of his reefs); and of 2. the univalency of "sail," which neglects "toile"'s second (esthetic) connotation. The selection of "canvas" is, I think, a better solution, as it functions much the same as Mallarmé's "toile": it may be a synecdoche for art, or else a "double" synecdoche, the canvas being the material of a sail, which figuratively represents the poetic boat. This leaves us with the final and equally interesting problem of rhyme ("star"/"canvas"?). "Canvas" is not an easy word to rhyme, but among the possibilities in the "star family," the only word that offers at least an off-rhyme is "asterisk." Now at first this may seem a bizarre choice, since it is not a "real" star, if we are to stick to literal meanings. But we must remember that Mallarmé did *not* and was in constant consultation with the *Littré* dictionary for shades of meanings, ambiguities, etymological nuances, etc. The following rumination, justifying the off-rhyme finally selected, may well reflect the type of thinking Mallarmé did as he selected *his* "étoile." "Asterisk" (another meaning of the French "étoile"), from the Greek *asteriskos*, means, literally, "little star." But "étoile" is not meant simply as a "real" star in the poem (i.e., poems should be *about* stars, although we *do* see them constantly—alone and in constellations—in Mallarmé's poetry), but rather as a symbol of a search "on high" that guides the poet (his quest for the ideal, etc.). Thus, "étoile" is also endowed with an essential and undeniable figurative quality (as is the "récif"), which, we discover, "asterisk" shares. The latter word has, as its primary meaning, "a starlike sign used in printing and writing as a reference to a passage or a note in the margin, or to fill the space where words are omitted." And what better *figurative* description could there be of Mallarmé's poetic quest? The "asterisk," as the "étoile," thus suggests a *substitution for words* (words omitted or words outside the text), the perfect, pure solution to the problem of the impurity of words, which was the fundamental defect Mallarmé sought to efface through his poetic alchemy and condensation. Perhaps not by coincidence, we shall, in fact, witness this same phenomenon in practice when we read *"Ses purs ongles très haut dédiant leur onyx..."*: there, the words in the poem self-destruct, as do the objects described, leaving nothing to survive but... the "scintillations of the septuor," the twinklings of the *stars* in the Big Dipper.

LA CHEVELURE VOL D'UNE FLAMME...

One of Mallarmé's late sonnets, this poem originally appeared in the body of a prose poem, "La Déclaration foraine." It is typical of Mallarmé's late, elliptical style; but it is exceptional in that it is in the Shakespearean sonnet form (three quatrains and a distich), and it does not treat the cosmic drama of the void or the poet's own drama of writing poetry, but rather deals with another protagonist (a woman) and is a poem of celebration. What it celebrates, in a series of images of fire and light, is the magnificent glory of a woman (probably Mallarmé's friend, Méry Laurent, but this biographical fact is beside the point of the poem itself, of Mallarmé's expression). She is portrayed (or rather sketched, in the poet's typically suggestive manner) as a regal, glowing personage whose beauty (outer and inner) seems to transcend her own sensuality and the poet's desires (vv. 2, 9). It is significant that the woman is never mentioned by name; indeed, she is never even mentioned. All that we see of her are the synecdochical flashes of hair, eye, finger, and head. The "plot" (again, such an effort to simplify the poem "defames" it: cf. v. 9) is nothing more than the description of the female presence. The opening stanza presents the hair, flying up in flames and then being placed back on the brow. Next, it is hoped (by the poet?) that this "inner fire," initially in the hair, continues to glow in the woman's eye, whether sincere or mocking (of the poet?). The poet's nudity is then subordinated to the woman's magnificence, unadorned (v. 10), which (and now we return to the hair, in the final three verses), again as flaming torch, accomplishes the heroic deed of allaying doubt (like chance, a constant figure in Mallarmé's poetry). If this "résumé" (cf., later, *"Toute l'âme résumée..."*) seems fragmented, it is because the poem is reduced to suggestion and scintillation, to elusive gesture and linguistic connotation.

The only formal change that has been made (in the interest of rhyme) is that the quatrains are in *rimes embrassées*, not *rimes croisées*. That Mallarmé has chosen "chevelure" (and not "cheveux") as the focal word of the text is significant. "Chevelure" suggests an ensemble of hair, not hair generally. Further, the word may be used as the "tail" of a comet. (As we have seen in Corbière's "Petit mort pour rire," the source of the word for "comet" is the Greek word for hair, "komé.") My "combèd hair" both describes the specific hair here (it is being combed by the female presence, arranged into a "crown"—confirmed by the "diadème" of v. 3—on her brow) and is a near-homonym of "comet," which allows the "chevelure" to retain its polyvalent status as comet and hair. This also allows the English text, as the French one, to begin with the astral motif ("La chevelure vol..." or "The combèd hair flight...")—which adorns the woman with a celestial radiance— continued by the expressions "nue" (v. 5) and "astre" (v. 10). The *enjambement* is retained throughout the entire first stanza. "Ancien foyer" (v. 4) is rendered as "original hearth." I have selected this adjective over other possibilities ("ancient" or "former"), as it gives the impression not of a temporal displacement, but, rather, of a spatial one: the hair is returned, in a cyclical movement, back to the brow, after having flared up. (The desire to "unfurl it all" has ceased as the woman places it back to its original place, in braids, on the brow.) This movement *back* to the original spot is suggested both by the "diadem," the form of a crown/flight, and by the cosmic cycle of sunrise/sunset, seen in the word "Occident." "Hearth" (not "home") was chosen because the French "foyer" suggests both "home" and "fire" (from the Latin *focus*, "fireplace"): indeed, we suspect this was the reason behind Mallarmé's choice of this ambiguous word, as the motif of fire is essential to the poem's imagery (cf. vv. 1, 6, 10, 12, 13, 14). "Sigh" (v. 5) is, as the poem's context strongly suggests, an imperative (the poet speaking to himself, or perhaps to the reader), and not an antecedent-less infinitive. "Cloud alive" is inverted because of the French anteposed adjective; the by-product is an assonant-rhyme with v. 8. As in the opening verse of *"A la nue accablante tu...,"* the possibility of "nue"'s being a naked woman is faint, but unlikely (here, it is the *hero*'s nudity that defames the ethereal nature of the woman); and, further, this would necessitate the choice of the nonexistent English word that encompasses both "cloud" and "naked woman." In the next verse, I have used "ever" instead of "still" or "always" (all three are possible) for the purpose of adding a third *r* sound. (There are also three in the French "toujou*r*s inté*r*ieu*r*.") "Persevere" has much the same sense as "continue" and was selected for the consonant-rhyme (with "fire"); it is, as is the French "continue," in the subjunctive mode.

(Some have, wrongly I think, suggested that "continue" is the feminine form of the adjective "continu.") The "feux" of v. 10 may be jewels (on the woman's finger) or even stars, but not literal "fires." It is the metonymic heat of the flames that is stressed in my version, consistent with the French usage, as well as the retaining of an assonant-rhyme with v. 12. The twelfth verse presents the poem's greatest challenge to the translator. First, "fulgurante" is translated as "with flames / Of lightning," allowing the rhyme with v. 9 and conjoining the motif of fire (already established) with the visual effect of the woman's "flashing." Moreover, in the French, the displaced "fulgurante," modifying "femme" (or even "Celle") but juxtaposed curiously with the masculine "chef," creates a typically Mallarméan syntactical confusion. As this confusion is impossible to recreate in English (there are no genders for substantives in this language), I have instead created a *different* confusion in its place: the consecutive "with"'s of the eleventh verse. Mallarmé's (deliberate) use of the archaic "chef" for "tête" is also a problem. The English "head" would simply give the modern semantic equivalent, which would not differentiate the actual use of "chef" from the alternate (rejected) use of "tête." In English, there are, in fact, three *old* forms of the word that would approximate the archaic French usage: the Anglo-Saxon *heafod* and two Middle English forms, *heved* and *hed*. Of these, the first two are too esoteric, since the French reader *would* recognize "chef" as an old form of "tête," whereas the English reader would not be able to decipher either *heafod* or *heved*. *Hed*, on the other hand, is both archaic and recognizable, because it is close in spelling to, and a homonym of, "head." In the same verse, "feat" would have been a better rhyme with "heat" than "deed." (They both translate the meaning of "exploit.") But the former choice would have produced an inappropriate (and unfortunate) pun as a result of its juxtaposition with "hed" ("hed"/ "feat"). "Torch" (v. 14) can only be retained if the previous verse ends in "would scorch." The problems here are the conditional tense (for the rhyme: "scorches"/"torch" will not do) and the inaccuracy of "scorch" (for "flay" or "graze" or "skin"). "Flays"/"blaze" is my solution, both retaining the rhyme and the semantic accuracy of "écorche" and substituting "blaze" for "torch" (which still repeats the "flame" image begun in the opening verse of the poem). Finally, "Just like" is chosen over "Like" (as, in the French, "Ainsi qu' " replaces the more common "Comme") to add the needed beat to the tetrameter.

SAINTE

Mallarmé wrote this poem for Cécile Brunet, wife of Jean Brunet (a Félibrige poet) and godmother of Mallarmé's daughter, Gene-viève. The occasion is the feast day of Mme Brunet's patronym, Cé-cile, saint of music. But as in *"La chevelure vol d'une flamme…,"* the biographical data should not distract us from the essential—the poem, which stands alone, independent of any source or model. This is perhaps the purest of all of Mallarmé's poems, a piece reduced to a bare minimum, to a skeleton of structural echoes and suggestion. Its title, originally "Sainte Cécile jouant sur l'aile d'un chérubin," was elliptically reduced to a simple "Sainte." There is only one main verb in the entire poem (v. 5), the frail third-person singular of the verb *être*, which merely signals the Saint's existence. But "existence" is an elusive term here, as this poem, like so many of Mallarmé's, is one of non-existence as well, of absence and silence. As in *"Toute l'âme ré-sumée…"* and *"Ses purs ongles très haut dédiant leur onyx…,"* the objects in the poem self-destruct, leaving us with the sounds, the phrasing, and the suggestive web of words that lay tantalizingly on the white sheet of paper. The first two stanzas are nearly identical in structure, with present participles, postposed adjectives, relative pronouns, reflexive verbs, prepositions, adverbs, and substantive pairs, respectively, placed in parallel positions. We look at a window (apparently stained-glass), where there are depicted viola, flute, mandora (stanza 1), and Saint and hymnal (stanza 2). But the instruments are cancelled out by the verb *receler* and the adverb "jadis"; and although the Saint is there (for the moment: her status as "musician" [of sounds] disap-pears in the final verse), the hymnal is silenced by "jadis" and will later disappear in v. 14 (introduced by the negativizing "sans"), giving way to the angel's wing. What remains in the stanzas is the structure alone, without any referents save the Saint. The colon in v. 8 introduces a two-stanza-long qualification: the Saint in the window appears to be accompanied by an angel whose wing (described metonymically as an "evening flight": it does not fly at all, suggesting *absence* of function, just as the Saint is a musician, not of sounds, but of silence) serves as an instrument for the Saint. But she does not play it: by now, the real instrument (viola) and hymnal have vanished, and the wing is not played, but merely balanced—between being and non-being, sound and silence, hanging by the thinnest thread of its own structure and suspended words.

What is most essential in the translation of this poem is the preserva-tion of form: especially in the opening two stanzas, I have tried to retain the precise word order and rhyme. Concerning the latter, I have come close to Mallarmé's schema: his rhymes are ABAB/ACAC; mine are A^1BA^2B/A^1BA^2B. (Both "A" rhymes are present participles, but each rhyme has in addition its shared vowel sound preceding the participle ending.) In both the original and my version, the two quatrains are given three different rhymes (and not the usual two or four). An unexpected, often undetected, but no less interesting problem is that of the unassuming word "vieux" (vv. 2, 6, 13, 14). In the first two instances, the adjective (uncharacteristically) follows its modified substantive, and in the final quatrain, the order is reversed (or returned to normal). The purpose of the inversion in vv. 2 and 6 (as in the title of Corbière's "Paysage mauvais") is to emphasize a specific trait, here the aging process of the nearly-defunct (and, furthermore, "concealed") wood and hymnal. They are, at the poem's conclusion, merely "old," but at that point they are not being described (or "non-described"!) in terms of their physical presence, but rather in terms of their absence (introduced by "sans"). I have used "ancient" in the first two instances and "agèd" in the second two: not only does this underline the graded semantic nuances resulting from the change in syntax (rather than inverting, which would, of course, not work in English: "santal old"... "old santal"), but, by rejecting "old," it also presents the reader with a nearly homonymic pair ("ancient"/"agèd"), which is a close approximation of the use of identical (although syntactically variant) expressions ("vieux"/"vieux") in the French. "Viol" is used instead of "viola" in v. 3: this "old" form of the word for the stringed instrument is more appropriate to the "context of yore"— Saint Cecilia, the stained-glass window, the ancient hymnal, etc. In addition, it retains, with "santal," the sounds of the terminal *l*'s of the original ("santal"/"viole"), placed, as are most of the words in the opening stanzas, in parallel positions in vv. 2-3. "Mandola" or "mandora" are both possible renderings for the "mandore" of v. 4: I have selected the former word, as the latter would have produced an undesired effect of cacophony in the English ("mandora of yore"). As with other words in the poem (and absent words omitted by the use of ellipsis and synecdoche), Mallarmé has compressed "vêpre et complie" (v. 8) to a bare minimum by using their singular forms. (They are always in the plural: "vêpres," "complies.") I have thus chosen the unusual form "vesper"; and, for the latter expression, I have selected "complin" over the alternative "compline," as the former is the *sparer* form in regard to number of letters. The inversion of subject and verb in the relative clause (v. 9) is a common "technique of confusion" employed by Mallarmé (cf. v. 4 of *"Ses purs ongles très haut dédiant leur onyx..."*). I have retained this inverted syntax; since the English "that" does not announce (as the French relative does) whether its antecedent is subject or object of the clause, my retaining the original syntax substitutes a different confusion factor: both "harp" and "window-light" may be the subject, since physically they are brushing each other. (That is, the wing is on the very surface of the glass.) "Harp" is thus allowed to contribute the consonant-rhyme with "tip." The off-rhyme "balances"/"silence" (vv. 14, 16) might have been avoided with the rhyme "positions"/"Silence's musician," but "Musician of silence" must be retained in the final verse, since "silence" must be the poem's final, nullifying echo, as it is Hamlet's.

This is a typically Mallarméan poem about the (internal and cosmic) drama of the process of writing poetry, the dialectics of presences and absences, of lightness and darkness, of victory and defeat. Unlike many of Mallarmé's poems, however, this piece leans more toward the affirmation of the poet's pride than the confirmation of his defeat. The inevitable law of death and darkness may menace the age-old dream of poetic creation—a dream typically ambivalent, based on desire and pride yet inevitably on suffering and defeat as well—but it cannot make the poet doubt its existence. (Although the "wing" of v. 4 is folded in quiet resignation, it still exists and affirms itself: cf. the proud swan/poet's situation in *"Le vierge, le vivace et le bel aujourd'hui..."*) Splendid night, the cosmic setting of the poet's drama, with its stars consuming themselves (as stars do), cannot compare to the splendor of the solitary poet's faith, which emanates from the Earth, obscuring it (Earth) less through the passing of time; indeed, the stars are there (in all their "vileness") simply to confirm the existence of the only true light—the genius of the earthling-poet. This résumé, of course, once again cannot capture the poem itself: only the latter can do that. But the discussion of some of the problems the translator faces may help to "illuminate" the power and beauty of this extraordinary poem.

"Menaced" must be in the past tense, not the imperfect, as the opening conjunction might suggest: "menaced" thus corresponds to the French *passé simple*. Ellipsis has been retained in v. 2 ("Such old dream") to preserve the spare quality of the odd French locution that expresses the absolute and ongoing nature of the poet's "Dream." The literal "vertebrae" (or even "spine"?) may be a better choice than "feeling" at the conclusion of the second verse. Although my motive was primarily to retain the only rhyme possible (with "ceilings," to keep the ABBA rhyme intact), it should be noted that "vertèbres" (which in fact stands between paralysis and "feeling," in the physical sense) is to be taken in its figurative sense of "marrow," "essential being" (as poet). This essential self-as-poet corresponds more to the affective or intuitive powers of the poet than his physical presence. "Indubitable," learned and seemingly pompous, is an odd word to use in a poetic text, but altogether typical of Mallarmé's lexicon; it is the only effective word to use in this situation to express the absolute presence of the poetic "feeling" or Dream. I have thus preserved this connotation by a literal rendering. On the other hand, "throes" (v. 6) is selected over the more literal "death": the stars are constantly *in the process of* dying (as we shall see in the flickering throes of the constellation ["agonise"] in v. 10 of *"Ses purs ongles très haut dédiant leur onyx..."*); and, further, the word preserves the sounds of Mallarmé's sixth verse—whereas he uses open *o* sounds as assonance, I have substituted *t/th* sounds as consonance. Conversely, my choice of "belied" (for "menti") substitutes the effect of assonance ("pri*de* beli*e*d") for his repetition of consonants in the same verse ("men*ti*... *t*énèbres"). The "solitaire" of v. 8 demands a special explanation. In French, as in English, it may be used as both adjective and, as here, substantive. The literal rendering preserves the three possible meanings, all appropriate to the context. It may refer to the "lone" poet, whose status is that of a recluse, separated from humanity by his lonely drama of creation. The word also suggests a single diamond, confirmed by the adjective "ébloui," as well as the "éclat" of v. 10, the "astre en fête" of v. 14, and the general motif of dazzling brightness represented by poetic genius. Third, it suggests the card game: the "jeu" is, of course, the supreme game of poetry, which attempts, however futilely, to overcome the omnipotent and omnipresent rules (cf. the "fatale loi" of v. 1) of chance, of the *hasard* of language. (Significantly, *hasard* is a game as well, played with dice: this form of "jeu" will reappear constantly, most notably in Mallarmé's final tribute to the cosmic poetic drama, "Un coup de dés.") "Afar from," not "far from" (v. 9) more closely reflects the "au lointain de" (not "loin de") of the original. Verse 10 is inverted, as in the French, to emphasize the strangeness, the inhabitual nature of the poet's dazzling powers. "Mystery strange" has also been inverted, to underline the force of the adjective: it appears in the unusual anteposed position in the French. The happy by-product is the rhyme with v. 12. In v. 12, what is suggested is that space—depending on theories of expansion and entropy—either expands or contracts. For the latter concept, the verb "se nie" may be rendered as "denies itself" or "contracts itself." But a third option, the "derange" I have chosen, has the sense of "puts itself out of order," which, in this cosmic context, is appropriate to the relativity and orientation of space itself. "As witness" (v. 13) is selected rather than "to witness" ("pour témoins"): in the French, the substantive is used—an unusual construction—in a verbal sense (for "pour *témoigner* / Que"). The "as" preserves the strangeness of the construction as well as preserving the substantive/verb status of "witness." The syntax of the final verse *should be* "le génie d'un astre en fête s'est allumé": Mallarmé has chosen both to displace the auxiliary from its past participle and to invert the subject/verb sequence. His purpose is both to disorient and to save for the final words of the poem the juxtaposed expression "allumé le génie." I have preserved this strange syntax in my version, since this procedure—seen elsewhere in, for example, the conclusions of *"Le vierge, le vivace et le bel aujourd'hui..."* and *"Ses purs ongles très haut dédiant leur onyx..."*—is essential to Mallarmé's dramatic structuring of the poem.

LE VIERGE, LE VIVACE ET LE BEL AUJOURD'HUI...

This is perhaps Mallarmé's most celebrated sonnet, and it is one of the great "swan" poems in the French tradition, along with Baudelaire's "Le Cygne." Again, for the (misleading but reassuring) purposes of clarification and orientation, I shall first present a brief "summary of what is going on here." The poet asks if "today" will break through the ice haunted by a glacier. (The "asking" is nearly rhetorical, however: we note, in v. 4, the substitution of an exclamation point for the expected question mark.) Both "glacier" and "today" turn out to be a swan stuck in the ice and trying to escape from his frigid imprisonment. But the swan cannot—indeed, does not wish to—escape and is fixed in this hopeless, but scornfully proud isolation. After close readings (we note, for example, the significance of expressions such as "chanté," "stérile," "pur éclat," "songe froid de mépris," "exil inutile," and a capitalized "Cygne"), we discover that the poem's real (and, for Mallarmé, familiar) subject is not simply the plight of a pathetic winged creature, but the dialectical situation of the poet (the swan is, after all, a traditional symbol of the poet), divorced from the common scribe in his painful and sterile quest for perfection, but proud of his uniqueness and isolation. As usual, the essence of the poem is not this "plot," but rather the drama of mystery and suggestiveness buried within the words themselves. In fact, the reader is obliged to ask questions after virtually every word of the sonnet (e.g., "why 'enduring'?"; "which glacier?"; "which flights?"; "why the exclamation point?"; "frigid dream of scorn?"; "why is the final *C* capitalized?"; and so on), to struggle with the elusive language from beginning to

end. And this is where the discussion of the translation becomes significant, for it may well bring us closer to the text's essence: not as an
explication of what is taking place, but as a guide to a better understanding of the problems and questions that a careful reading of this
frustratingly dense poem elicits.

As with the reading of any poem by Mallarmé, paraphrasing is ill-
advised. Thus, "today" of v. 1 must remain as is. Similarly, words as
unobtrusive and seemingly insignificant as the three definite articles
of this opening verse must be retained, because in the original text the
entire verse leads up to the startling surprise of the single, simple final
word: "aujourd'hui." It is a surprise, as we discover that this abstract
word, ordinarily an adverb, is in fact the subject of the entire first
stanza (and of the rather physical verb *déchirer*). "Vierge" and "vivace"
might have been, because with their accompanying definite articles,
they may be construed, until the appearance of "bel aujourd'hui," as
being not only adjectives, but also as adjectives become substantives. I
have chosen "beauteous" for "bel" (instead of the usual "beautiful" or
"lovely"): because "bel," by its unusual form (only used before masculine singular nouns)—which tips off "aujourd'hui"'s status as
substantive—is incongruous with the other two preceding adjectives,
"beauteous," by its archaic formation, offers a corresponding condi-
tion of incongruity. The second verse in French manifests an obvious
series of *i* sounds, inserted by Mallarmé throughout the entire poem
in order to create a hauntingly sonorous unity. To the French "*il*...
déch*i*rer... *i*vre" corresponds my "sh*ea*r... f*e*verish... w*i*ng," explaining the choice of the first two expressions over other possible alternatives (e.g., "break," "shatter"; "drunk," "inebriated"). "Transparent"
and "glacier" are inverted, as in the French, to emphasize the strange
usage of the adjective. The oxymoron in v. 6 ("sans espoir se délivre,"
"without hope frees himself") intimates not an actual liberation, but
the attempt to escape (which, with both the swan *and* the poet, is—
willfully—abortive): thus, the choice of "strives / To escape," which,
conveniently, produces the off-rhyme "strives"/"live." "Live," like "today," must be presented as is and not paraphrased: the *life* of ordinary poets is here contrasted with the sterility inflicted on the poet.
The eighth verse is particularly noteworthy in terms of the problems
it presents to the reader and translator. The latter is often tempted to
avoid the obvious awkwardness of the English that I have carefully
attempted to maintain. In this case, it seems to me that an attempt to
make a "correct," "flowing" translation of the dislocated, inverted
French verse does the original text a disservice. The syntax of my

English version not only preserves the inversion of noun and possessive in the French (in both cases, the normal syntactic sequence noun/possessive/verb becomes possessive/verb/noun, to accent the "ennui" by placing it at the end of the verse), but it also maintains the juxtaposition—evocatively sonorous—of the "resplendi l'ennui": "gleamed the ennui." "Disannex" (v. 9) seems equally strained, especially with the more literal alternative, "shake off." But Mallarmé has slipped in a subtle pun: "Tout son col secouera." "Secouera," future tense of *secouer*, has the homonym "ce cou" embedded in it: thus, "tout son col, ce cou," "his whole neck, this neck." "Disannex" is not the ideal solution, but it does come close (albeit in a slightly Brooklynese English) to preserving the original word play: "His whole neck, [dis...neck]." "White" and "agony" are inverted—again, at the expense of "not sounding right"—to preserve the conscious inversion by Mallarmé, which emphasizes the *white* agony of the desolate, sterile setting (the topographical analogue to the sterile whiteness of the page, already seen in the final verse of "Salut"). The final tercet attempts to reproduce, in approximate form, the *i* sounds of the original French: there are no fewer than eleven *i* sounds in the French and sixteen various *i* sounds in English. "Indicts," although not precisely parallel to the French "assigne" ("assigns"), both suggests the punitive element of the swan/poet's imprisonment and contributes to the sonorous ambience (especially as a rhyme) of the stanza. As does "fixes himself," which, in addition to the two *i* sounds, retains the *reflexive* quality of the French verb (as opposed to an alternative translation, "is fixed": but cf. the difference, in context *and* translation, of a similar reflexive verb, in v. 13 of "*Ses purs ongles très haut dédiant leur onyx...*"): we should not forget, after all (vv. 10-11), that this horrible exile is a proudly self-imposed one. "Frigid," for "cold," performs the same sonorous function. I have placed it at the end of the verse, and not before its modified substantive, as it is one of the few possible (assonant-)rhymes with "Cygnet": there is no sacrifice, since, in context, this adjective clearly modifies "dream." "Adorns," for the more literal "clothes," contributes internal rhyme (with "scorn": it is followed by "futile exile") and alliteration (with "amidst") to the tercet. For dramatic reasons, the word for swan must be the final one of the sonnet, as it is in the French: it is the final appearance of the bird, now apotheosized (as is Baudelaire's swan in "Le Cygne") from a mere beast to a *symbol* of the poet's situation. As such, it is a sort of "sign," and Mallarmé has been careful not only to capitalize the word, but also to suggest the symbolic status of the bird by the implied homophonic pair "Cygne"/"Signe" ("Swan"/"Sign"). This is not possible in English, except if we use the word "Cygnet," with its own *corresponding* homonym, "Signet," a sort of sign, literally the poet's own "stamp" or "signature." In fact, "Cygnet" and "signet" are precisely parallel, since they are etymologically diminutives, "cygnet" of the swan, and "signet" of the sign (literally, a "small sign"). What is to be gained here (reflection of the lexical ambiguity of the original, as well as the addition of yet another *i* sound) is a good example of, and well worth, the (relatively small) sacrifice of *meaning*. (Mallarmé's swan is presumably a full-grown bird, not a young one.)

SES PURS ONGLES TRÈS HAUT DÉDIANT LEUR ONYX...

One of the Master's great *tours de force*, commonly referred to as the "sonnet en -yx." This represents *the* essential Mallarmé, a poem in which the slight objects chosen for the "subject" disappear, one by one, leaving, at the end, the high and mysterious drama of the cosmic void (here, as in "Un coup de dés," in the form of a constellation). The "plot" consists of the description of what is in the poet's ("le Maître"'s) room: a "torchbearer" (a statue of one?), holding not a torch but an abstraction (evening dreams) burned by the Phoenix (traditionally the burn*ee*!), without, however, leaving any ashes to be collected by some urn or another; credences (even though the parlor is empty!); and, on them, *no* "ptyx," which itself can't exist, because it doesn't mean anything, being a word—from the Greek "fold"—made up by Mallarmé for the rhyme (more on that later...). The "Master" (poet?) of the abode isn't even there, as he has absconded with his make-believe ptyx to fill it up with tears from the Styx (in Hades: a bizarre voyage for a mortal). In the tercets, the window is vacant; the light (only "one"...?) is dying, reflecting only "perhaps" on the decor; the nix (a pattern? a statue? a figment?) has died; the mirror is but nothingness; and all that is left is the reflection in the mirror of the twinkling of the Big Dipper, the cosmic result of the nix's (Calisto's) transformation. If this is all confusing,... it is. What Mallarmé has done is to describe *nothing* in exquisitely evanescent, elusive terms, so that what is left—as is so often the case—is simply the words, their relationship with each other, their sounds, their suggestive power, in short, their *own* drama. We should also notice the sparseness of the poem's rhyme: only two rhymes are used in the French, and most rare ones at that ("yx," "or"). I have tried to approximate this conscious frugality but could do no better than to limit the English version to four rhymes: Mallarmé's poem is ABAB/ABAB/BBA/BAB; mine is ABAB/ACAC/DBA/DAB.

The first problem we encounter is the "lampadophore" of v. 2. Most translate this into its literal English equivalent, "torchbearer," probably because the term "lampadephore" may seem somewhat "literal" or "stiff." This, I believe, should at least be questioned. I have chosen to leave the expression intact, in order to preserve Mallarmé's original intent of infusing the poem with a classical ambience, appropriate to the cosmic and mythical drama that takes place at the conclusion. To this end, Mallarmé has used the expressions "lampadophore," "Phénix," "amphore," "ptyx," "Styx," "nixe," and the Latin "septuor." "Vesperal," not "vespertine" or "evening," as this choice presents the reader with the desired ambiguous connotations of both "evening" and "liturgical": the act of proffering the torch by the Greek figure is a quasi-religious one, confirmed by the other expressions "purs," "en haut," and "dédiant." The fourth verse also presents an interesting, somewhat complex problem, usually avoided (and, I believe, wrongly so) by a more "normal" syntax in translation. But the syntax in the French is *intended* to be confusing: Mallarmé has used neither "correct" clause—"*Qui* ne recueille pas de cinéraire amphore" ("That does not gather up any cinerary urn"), "Que ne recueille pas *une* [*la*] cinéraire amphore" ("That a [the] cinerary urn does not gather up"). Instead, the subject of the clause (the "urn," which does not collect its object, the many vesperal dreams) is introduced by "de," which serves two purposes: it (consciously) renders indefinite (as do other favorite words of Mallarmé's, like "tel" and "quelque": see, e.g., *"Toute l'âme résumée…,"* v. 5) the specific identity of any one particular urn; and it creates the syntactic illusion of there not even *being* an urn there at all, by its placement after the word "pas" ("pas de…" denotes absence of quantity). In the English version, the "not any" preserves this ambiguity, as the reader may pause either after the "not" (the "any" then modifies the urn, and the "not" negates the "gathers up") or after "up" (the "not any," then, as the "pas de," suggests total absence of urn). "Amphora," not "urn," for the same reasons as applied to "lampadephore." Further, the sonority of *"any* cine*rary* amph*ora"* is very close to the same element in the French (as opposed, for example, to something like "no cinerary urn"). "Credences," not "credenzas" (v. 5), maintains the religious, ceremonial ambience mentioned above. ("Plot-wise," it hardly matters, since these tables aren't there anyway in this "empty parlor.") "Ptyx" is chosen for "conch" or "pleat": not only does this retain the Greek (mythical) flavor (along with "lampadephore," etc.), but it seems useless to paraphrase a word that does not exist and has no real (denotative) meaning. The sixth verse is particularly challenging, since the French presents such a curiously "untranslatable" problem. Mallarmé's verse—a description of, and in apposition to, the "ptyx"—*means* absolutely nothing, and in fact it suggests the "nihility" of the "ptyx" by the absence of sense and the presence of but (cacophonous) sound, appropriate to a meaningless entity. All that remains in the verse is the echoing of the letters: b-o-l-i/b-i-b-l-o//i-n-n/o-n-o. The more pressing problem is to reproduce the sound patterns of the first hemistich. "Abolished bibelot" or "Abolished bauble" is the traditional route, but somehow (since sound, not meaning, is paramount here) the alliance of the two words in English—due to the change in sound and in tonicity—loses the effect that it has in the French. What my "Nullified knickknack" does is to replace "bibelot" with a word quintessentially sonorous (cacophonous) and semantically void—"knickknack"—and, even more, to come closer to reproducing the sound pattern of the French: for the three *b*'s, two *l*'s, two *i*'s, and two *o*'s in French, it offers three *n*'s, two *k*'s, and two *i*'s (in addition to the strangeness of four *k*'s in a single word, two of them uselessly silent, to compensate somewhat for the sonorous inferiority of the traditional English version). The ninth verse also needs to be carefully considered. The "incorrect" grammar is a conscious device Mallarmé uses to make the sense (and the reading) difficult and compressed: it *should* be "Mais proche *de* la croisée *vacante au nord*, de l'or...." (But, of course, it isn't, and that is why Mallarmé is a great poet and this "correct" verse is inferior.) "Next the," instead of "Next to the," captures this willed inaccuracy and conscious concision; "vacant" is displaced in my English version; and "karat" replaces the synecdochical "un or" (for "de l'or") with a synecdoche of its own: "karat" for "gold." (This usage is in contrast, for instance, to the "sans or"—"without gold"—of v. 5 of *La chevelure vol d'une flamme..."*). A few words are in order concerning the last two word choices. "Vacant," in addition to being very close in meaning to the French (the "casement," or window, is empty, functionless, belonging to no one—a void, as is all else in the poem: "void" or "empty" would reduce these various connotations to a single meaning), replaces the obvious echo of the French "au nord... un or" with its own, "casement... vacant." I might have, as is customary, used "a gold" for "un or" (they are *both* unusual usages); but not only does "karat" offer the same synecdochical effect (in fact, it may even be more effective), but the resultant uncommon rhyme ("karat"/"whereat") appropriately reflects the difficult rhyming of the original. The final verse sounds somewhat stilted in English. But "unstiffening the French" would, again, betray the essence of the original. "So soon" (not "as soon" or "right away") is equivalent to the same confusion created by "sitôt" (which suggests the temporal simultaneity of the death of the nix and the appearance of the constellation in the mirror). More important, it maintains the play of *s* sounds, which, as in v. 6, replaces any meaning or action. Hence, the similar retention of the sounds in "scintillations" and "septuor." For the latter, "Dipper" would be a litteral transposition, sacrificing the sound effect. "Septuor" does four things: retain the *s* sound; retain the rhyme in "or" of the original; retain the classical terminology (here, Latin) desired by Mallarmé; and suggest the element of Music (septuor is also synonymous with "septet" in English), which, as an esthetic analogue to poetry (a fond comparison of Mallarmé's and, in fact, a hallmark of all "Symbolist" verse), is, after all, the *raison d'être* of this, as of every poem the Master ever wrote.

LE TOMBEAU DE CHARLES BAUDELAIRE

Despite the judgments of some who criticize it as being overly turgid, this poem is a wonderful example of Mallarmé's art of suggestion and a sincere and perceptive homage to a poet who had a profound effect on his own writing. It is eclectic in that it evokes the various themes of Baudelaire's poetry (spleen, spirituality, alchemy, the city, prostitution, female hair, sexuality, etc.) as well as many oblique allusions to specific poems ("Correspondances," "Crépuscule du soir," "La Chevelure," "Crépuscule du matin," "Le Vin des chiffonniers"). But more than being an homage to Baudelaire, it captures the essence of this great poet, while retaining all the elusiveness of Mallarmé's own expression. The poem is imbued with the major theme of *Les Fleurs du Mal*—the dialectic of good and evil. In the first two stanzas, spirituality and lubricity, the two poles of the moral spectrum, are posited by Mallarmé as the complementary forces of Baudelaire's poetry, each presenting its own paradox. The first stanza suggests the contrast between ancient spirituality (the buried temple, the dog-god idol Anubis) and sacrilege ("sewer-mouth," "slobbering," "slop," "abominably," "ferocious yelp"). There is, moreover, the juxtaposition of "boue" and "rubis," intimating the alchemy of Baudelaire's poetry ("Tu m'as donné ta boue et j'en ai fait de l'or") and the essential polarity of *spleen* and *idéal*. The "Ou" of v. 5 introduces the other side: a modern setting this time, a picture of Paris with its recent gas-lamps, the context of Baudelaire's *Tableaux parisiens* in particular. The paradox here is that the "shady" side of the city explored by Baudelaire (the "mèche" suggests either the modernity of the lamps or the—synecdochical—hair of the prostitutes who people *Les Fleurs du Mal*, perhaps even Jeanne Duval specifically: this possibility is confirmed by vv. 7-8) reveals, through its depravity and insults heaped upon it, a certain spirituality and redemptive quality: the—again synecdochical—pubic area of the female is immortal. In the tercets, Mallarmé pays homage to Baudelaire's shade, whose shroud-less presence alone—and not any votive wreath—can be the appropriate tombstone tribute. The very shade of the poet is, for us, Baudelaire's legacy, to be savored through the poetry, despite the latter's "sacrilege" and (morally) destructive qualities. (The tone here is, of course, ironic.)

The poem is a perfect illustration of the fundamental problem I have discussed in this volume's Introduction: the *misguided* temptation to render a difficult, intentionally elliptical and disjointed text into a fluid, clear, syntactically coherent one. The results of this practice would, of course, destroy the integrity and intent of the original poem. Consequently, I have avoided temptations such as the following: adding punctuation for clarity (commas at the end of vv. 3, 5, 6, and 13 and in the middle of vv. 5 and 13; a period at the end of v. 8; parentheses around "his very Shade," v. 13); filling in ellipses (changing "it" to "it could," v. 10; inserting "even" before "if," v. 14); and "normalizing" syntax (moving "Votif" to v. 9, "vainement" to v. 10, and "absente" to the beginning of v. 12). The inevitable criticism will be that the English version may thus seem "stiff": the reply is that it is meant to be so, to be faithful to Mallarmé's original poem. One of the sacrifices that has to be made in this regard is the poem's rhymes (it is—with *"À la nue accablante tu…"*—one of the most difficult of Mallarmé's poems to rhyme in English): my version is entirely in off-rhyme, with the exception of vv. 5 and 8. "Sepulchral" is placed at the end of the opening verse to retain the *enjambement* of Mallarmé's: "yelp" was, consequently, chosen over "bark" ("aboi") for the off-rhyme. In v. 2, "boue," literally "mud," becomes "slop" in my version. The reference here is, clearly, to Baudelaire's poetic alchemy, proposed in his famous comment, mentioned above: "Tu m'as donné ta boue et j'en ai fait de l'or." Whether this matter is "mud" or "slop" is unimportant, as long as the idea of some vile alchemical material (the starting point, to be transformed into gold, just as the vile material of Baudelaire's poems is transformed into beautiful expression) is understood. The advantage of the choice of "slop" is that this word retains both the *s* sound and the labial sound (*b* becomes *p* here) of the original. This is essential, as the cacophony of the stanza is a significant technique in suggesting the vile qualities of Baudelaire's poetic cosmos. (Are the *b*'s also chosen for… *B*audelaire?) In v. 5, the disorienting "Ou que" (not *"Où* que") introduces a verb in the subjunctive mode, "torde" (overlooked by many translators of this poem). The entire clause could be introduced, in English, by "let" or "that" or "if." I have chosen to render the clause as "the... gas twist the... wick as it might (, nonetheless)... It lights...," which both implies the essential idea that despite the wick's being twisted by gas (and wind, one supposes), the lamp still illumines the "immortal pubis"; and allows a rhyme with v. 8. "Shady" was chosen for "louche" (over other possibilities such as "shifty" or "suspicious") to retain the sounds of the French: "gaz... mèche louche" becomes "gas twist... shady." Further, the word "shady" contributes appropriately to the chiaroscuro effect of the light motif. "Absorbing" for "Essuyeuse" (v. 6), to suggest the two senses of the French expression: the (literal) wick absorbing the gas, and the phenomenon of Baudelaire's modernity (and his poetry in general) absorbing (figuratively) the insults of the public (or... the prostitute's hair absorbing abuse from the "proper" reader). "Abuse" was selected over "insults" ("opprobres") for the rhyme with the following verse. This rhyme ("abuse"/"pubis") was the only one possible: it may be termed "reversed assonance." "Haggard" must be retained, for its denotative meaning (pallor or even wildness, of the prostitute) as well as for its connotation, that of the "kept woman," resulting from the etymon *haga* ("hedge," suggesting falconry: the "kept woman" is also a creature of prey, like the falcon). The choice of "stealth" (v. 8) results from a more difficult problem. "Vol" may mean either "flight" (flitting from one lamppost to another) or "theft." The latter is not such a far-fetched possible connotation: cf. Baudelaire's "Crépuscule du soir," where evening is the "ami du criminel." "Stealth" both suggests the "shady" ("louche") movements of the woman and begins with "steal," which corresponds to the other meaning of "vol." "Sans soir" is "nightless" in my version, to retain (with "dried") the sonorous effects of the French. (Mallarmé's *s*'s become my *i*'s.) "Quarters" contributes to the rhyme (with "shudders," chosen over "shivers" for the rhyme) and corresponds to Baudelaire's "cités," not "cities," but Parisian "quartiers," perhaps "red light districts" where prostitutes "hang out all night" (v. 8). "Settle" (for "sit again"), consonant-rhyming with "marble," retains the ellipsis of the original: "comme elle [Ombre] [pourra] se rasseoir" becomes "as it [Shadow][could, to] settle." "Wreathes" (v. 12) was selected over "girds" or "binds" or "closes" or "surrounds," to suggest the contrast with the "vain" foliage of v. 9, the *wreath* placed on the poet's tomb, the form of which is round ("ceint"), like that of a belt. "Wreathes" thus connotes the act of "surrounding" (the shroud surrounds the absent Shade); the funereal ambience (cf. "feuillage"); and the *poetic* wreath, the "ceinture" of the laurel wreath.

I have, finally, chosen "destroys us" rather than the literal "if we die of it" (v. 14), for the assonant-rhyme with "poison" (v. 13).

TOUTE L'ÂME RÉSUMÉE...

This is one of the sparest of Mallarmé's sonnets, an *ars poetica* written on commission three years before his death. The central idea is a simple one: the writing of poetry should be based on the avoidance of "vile reality," of "too-precise meaning." The poet should ideally express himself by using vague, elusive, suggestive language. (Mallarmé had, very early on, written his friend Cazalis: "Peindre non la chose, mais l'effet qu'elle produit.") This "message" is embedded in a simile that compares the smoking of a cigar ("vile reality") in the first two quatrains to the writing (or "singing") of poetry in the third. (The transition word that is the simile's "fulchrum" is the "Ainsi" of v. 9.) Poetry is expressed just as the cigar is smoked—"savamment," "learnedly": in both cases, the "real" self-destructs. (We have already seen this phenomenon several times in previous discussions.) The cigar is "abolished" (its "soul," as poetry's) in several ways: the smoke is exhaled (and dies: *expirer* may mean "to die" as well) in smoke-rings that disappear one after the other; the cigar itself becomes ash, which is constantly in the act of leaving its burning ember, which, in fact, it once was. That is, what is left is the act of expiration (or exhalation), not what is "expressed" (the poem's "real subject"), as the latter disappears into ash and smoke. The words Mallarmé chooses throughout serve, in fact, to "abolish" the "real" subjects of the poem: "résumée" (the act of summarizing the soul is one of compression or concision, as is the act of writing poetry), "expirons," "abolis," "quelque" (the cigar is purposely left "vague," without the identity of an indefinite or definite article), "Brûlant," "se sépare," "vole-t-il," "exclus," "rature." It is also significant that the Shakespearean sonnet form is chosen. For what Mallarmé in fact does in the distich is to—literally—"abolish" the vagueness and suggestion of the first twelve verses by giving us an explicit, even didactic pair of verses that blatantly transgresses the very principles he has so carefully and "learnedly" implied up to that point. The too-precise vv. 13-14 "erase" the efforts of the entire poem.

I have had to alter the rhyme scheme, from Mallarmé's *rimes croisées* to my *rimes embrassées*. "Entire," not "whole," in the opening verse, was chosen for reasons of euphony: "whole soul" is slightly cacophonous. "Expire" (v. 2) retains both possible meanings of the French verb, the "death" of the soul into thin air and the smoker/poet's breathing (exhaling) it into rings. (Significantly, there is an etymological link between "âme" [soul] and "soupir" [breath].) "Spirals," suggesting the shape of smoke-rings, was selected over "rings" for the assonant-rhyme with "expire it." I have chosen "nullified" over "abolished" (v. 4), as in *"Ses purs ongles très haut dédiant leur onyx...,"* here for the assonant-rhyme with "summarized." "Learnedly" (v. 6) implies the linguistic sagacity (the adverb comes from the adjective "savant," suggesting scholarly activity) behind the cigar simile and inherent in the poetic enterprise: "knowingly" limits itself to a simple epis-temological sense. "Learnedly" also suggests (as does "savamment") the alchemical, secret element of Mallarmé's poetic activity, sym-bolized, in "Prose (pour des Esseintes)" and elsewhere, by the *grimoire*, the holy book of the magician/poet. "Dissever," synonymous with "sever," was chosen over the latter to preserve the rhythmic integrity of an already too-short verse. I have retained the term "romances" rather than (sentimental) "ballads": the former is closer to the original expression, calling attention to the specifically musical element of its poetic form. (It is juxtaposed with "chœur" and reveals Mallarmé's well-known conjunction of poetry and music.) "Hence" was relocated at the end of v. 9 (and used instead of "thus") for the rhyme with v. 11. "Volatiles" (v. 10) is the first of two neologisms—not present in the original—I have considered essential to use, despite their status as "non-words." (The other is the poem's final word, to be discussed below.) Here, the (English) transformation of adjective to verb calls attention to the word's "grammaticality," as does Mallarmé's "correct" formal grammar (the inversion of pronoun and verb—"vole-t-il"— after a short introductory adverb—"ainsi"). More important, the French "vole-t-il," carefully chosen, suggests "volatil": the two words are near-homonyms. The (implied) adjective confirms two elements of the poem—vapor (the smoke-rings abolishing themselves into thin air) and evanescence in general. The latter meaning is particularly important in the poem's context because of the "vague," imprecise poetry Mallarmé is defending. So "volatiles" (rather than the literal "flies") is a connotative choice, suggesting both *flight* (of poetry, and smoke, to the lips) and *dissipation* (smoke and poetry/music being volatile and self-destructing). "Because vile" (v. 12) retains the original ellipsis. The final words of both vv. 13 and 14 present the most in-triguing problem in translation and give us an insight into Mallarmé's word choice. Mallarmé used the same rhyme ("rature"/"littérature"), only reversed, in *Eventails*, X. If "vague littérature" is poetry that is, like smoke, self-abolishing, so is the very word "littérature": "litté" ("letters") + "rature" ("erase"). It seems to me that Mallarmé fully intended to suggest this phenomenon in the poem's final rhyme. "Rature" (v. 13), embedded in "littérature," must be rendered not as the figurative "destroys" or "ruins," but in its peculiarly *literary* sense of "erases." (The synonym in French is *biffer*, to cross out letters on a page: Mallarmé's obsession with black writing on the white page is well known.) So "erases," at the end of v. 13, must appear *within* (and at the end of) the final word of v. 14, thus preserving the Mallarméan word play ("rature"/"littérature," which is additionally a *rime million-naire* with five common phonemes). The only possibility for the poem's final word, then, is "literasure": it suggests the "correct" form ("literature"); (off-)rhymes with "erases"; and preserves the play on "erasure of letters" mentioned above. (A note: my original solution was to rhyme "litters" or even "belittles," v. 13, with "belles-lettres," v. 14; this was, for obvious reasons, far inferior.)

Une dentelle s'abolit...

One of Mallarmé's most complex poems, *"Une dentelle s'abolit..."* can hardly be subjected to a successful résumé. It is the third part of a "triptych of absence," in which the poetics of the void is given full expression. In this poem, the dialectics of absence/presence, creation/sterility, and music/silence are dominant. The illusory nature of the concrete world (the first two stanzas) is parallel to the poet's inner drama of the illusion of creativity (futile, but, in the final verse, potential). The first quatrain describes, or rather suggests, a decor consisting of a lace curtain half-revealing *no* bed (i.e., its function as curtain is denied). The "doute du Jeu suprême" has been variously interpreted as the vagueness of the dawn (God's Game); the Game of Love (suggested by the bed); and the Game of poetic creation. (To my mind, all three are possible, although the latter may be the most likely, in the context of the poem.) In the second stanza, the two parts of the curtain are specified, disappearing as they float against the dawn-flooded window. (It does not conceal anything, as the room in question seems to be empty.) After eight verses, then, nothing but light and fluttering lace is there; and the lace-network of words is dominated by expressions of absence. In the tercets, Mallarmé switches to the inner drama of the poet's dreams of creation, in which the "mandore" (which we have already seen in "Sainte")—representing the potentiality of music (poetry)—does not play, but rather sleeps in its "musical nothingness" (again, cf. the Saint, "Musicienne du silence") and, looking back to the window (of the quatrains, closing the comparison between the lace-drama and the mandola-drama: both dramas of the void), represents the potentiality of procreation (of sounds, but for the poet, who dreams this scene, of words: cf. the music/poetry linkage of *"Toute l'âme résumée..."*). This poem of the void thus ends on a note of hope and possibility, although the context of absence leaves scant hope for the gap between future and present to be bridged.

Since the actual language in this diaphanous piece is so very elusive, the problems of translation are, to a great extent, involved with capturing nuances of vagueness and connotation as well as retaining ellipsis, ambiguity, and carefully-planned sound patterns. The indefinite article of v. 1 must be retained, as it contributes to the lace's "abolition" (cf. other indefinites used by Mallarmé such as "tel" and "quelque," the latter appearing, for example, in *"Toute l'âme ré-sumée..."* and below, in v. 12). In the same (opening) verse, "plays dead" replaces a more literal choice such as "abolishes itself." First, the lace "feigns absence" ("plays dead") physically, in the Game of light that results in its "fading" against the equally pale window-pane, seen later in v. 7. Second, the lace "plays dead" in the sense of forfeiting its very function-as-lace (vv. 3-4, 8). Third, the "plays" of "plays dead" is consistent with the Mallarméan Game ("Jeu") in which the lace takes part. The choice of "But" for "Only" and the omission of any introductory article (v. 4) both help retain the desired rhythm of trimeter: the ellipsis is also purposely intended (part of Mallarmé's "Game" of compression). The two adjectives of v. 5 are inverted, as they are in the French. "Consolidated" (instead of, say, "evenly" or "totally") for "unanime" was chosen because 1. it denotes the "melding together" of the two curtains, explaining their "playing dead"; and 2. it has embedded within it "solid" (the lace, fading against the white pane and in the white light, is *solid* white). "Consolidated" reflects the same ambiguity as the French "unanime": it may be read either as an adjective, separate from "white," modifying "conflict" or as an adverb modifying "white." "Faded" (v. 7) suggests "fled" or "vanished" as well as the white color of the curtains *fading* into nothingness. "Pale pane," a normal choice, has the advantage over other possible ones of replacing the assonance in the French ("Enfu*i*"/"v*i*tre") with its own alliterative pattern. "Hides" was selected over "buries" (v. 8), both for the assonant-rhyme with v. 5 and to confirm the absence of function implied in vv. 3-4. My solution for the problematic "chez qui du rêve se dore" is "where dwells of dream the gilder." It is a problem because 1. "chez" is basically untranslatable (here, it may mean "at the home of," suggesting, as in *"Ses purs ongles très haut dédiant leur onyx...,"* the poet's abode; or "in whom," alluding to the poet's dream—of mandola or poetic expression); 2. Mallarmé has omitted the pronoun "celui" after "chez"; and 3. the inversion of the original, used for rhyme, must be retained (to do this in my version, I had to change the verb "gilds" into a substantive—"gilder"—for the off-rhyme with "mandola"). The "translated" equivalent (i.e., the literal, and *falsified* rendering) of the verse—solely for its sense—would be something like "at the home of [he] who gilds himself with dream." The sonorous effects of vv. 9-10 ("dore"/"dort"/"mandore") are partially recuperated (although the sounds are, of course, different) by the choice of "mandola" instead of "mandora," which gives to v. 10 another series of three identical sounds: "Sad*l*y"/"s*l*eeps"/"mando*l*a." (We recall that "mandola" was also chosen for the fourth verse of "Sainte," but in that case the reason was to avoid a cacophonous effect.) "Au creux néant musicien" presents the reader and translator with several problems. The first concerns the rhyme with v. 13. Rhyming an abstract word (meaning "nothingness," "the void," etc.) with "own" is possible if "néant" can mean, as it in fact does in context, "absence of sound" (not made by the musical/poetic instrument). Or… "no-tone." The second problem is a grammatical one: in French, both "creux" *and* "musicien" (carefully chosen here for their ambiguity) are words that may function either as adjective or substantive. The verse begins, moreover, with "Au," which often precedes the substantive "creux." We have, then, a verse with three (possible) consecutive substantives (although "néant" would be the prime syntactical choice). I have attempted to preserve this situation by choosing "lyric" over "musical": the former word may function as substantive or adjective (as alternative for "lyrical"). "Hollow," of course, functions as both as well. "Selon" (v. 13) *means* "according to," but in context it suggests a less abstract phenomenon (i.e., the birth of some sound from the mandola's belly). I have thus used "torn" (/"From") to suggest this (always potential) natal trauma. The expression is obviously too strong (as opposed to Mallarmé's curiously abstract preposition: he often employs "selon" to introduce a *spatial* element, as in v. 10 of *"Ses purs ongles très haut dédiant leur onyx…"*). But what is gained is the rhyme with "born" (v. 14) and the contribution of "torn" to the sonal pattern of the verse. Mallarmé's *"Telle que* vers *quelque* fenêtre"* thus becomes *"such that toward some* window *torn."*

A LA NUE ACCABLANTE TU…

Here is yet another little sonnet that cannot be paraphrased without spoiling the exquisite qualities of vagueness and ambiguity. The poem—another cataclysmic piece suggesting the drama of absence and the void—is marked by a series of negative or purposely indefinite expressions: "tu," "sans," "Quel," "abolit," "dévêtu," "faute," "quelque," "vain," "aura noyé." What has happened before the poem is written (thus, its "pretext") is not clear: the form of the poem is thus that of a double question. Under black foreboding clouds, what shipwreck transpired, the mast being the last (highest) part to sink? Or, if it wasn't a shipwreck, perhaps the ocean ("l'abîme") swallowed up the flank of a siren, having no "higher" disaster to account for? Hardly material for a "lofty" poem, we might say. But the résumé (as we expected) does not do the poem justice (in fact, it "abolishes" it!), since the very marrow of the poem is the "vague" subject in question and the corresponding manner in which it is expressed. The wreck is silenced; even the horn signalling the danger is "sans vertu" and cannot be witness; or, "hidden" by this possibility, the other "loss" is hardly likely, being that of a mythical being, the siren (cf. "Salut": the link between sirens and poetry is evident), and only her flank, at that. All that remains from the *hypothetical* cataclysm is not a bang but a whimper: the foam of the water. (The "cheveu" remains as well: hair of the siren? or, again, the white foam of the water?) As so often occurs in Mallarmé's verse, here again we see the barest evidence of "reality" remaining after all else has been "abolished." Thus, the action is but suggested, hinted at, and subordinated to the higher drama which is that of the void. The parallel drama of the poet struggling against the domination of the word and of *le hasard* is again the subcutaneous (tacit) subject of this difficult sonnet.

The preservation of suggestion and ambiguity from the French to the English is again the major challenge. In the opening verse, the first problem for the reader is the status of the "tu." In context, it is obviously the past participle of *taire* (modifying "naufrage"), but the potentiality of the personal pronoun always lurks in the background. I could not retain this nuance in English: from the possible semantic choices for the word (e.g., "stilled," "hushed," "silenced," "muted," "stifled," "muffled," "muzzled"), I have selected "checked," for the off-rhyme (with v. 3). This word is less accurate in suggesting the absence of the wreck's *sounds*, but the "trump" of v. 4 confirms that the "checking" of the wreck is auditory. "Basse" (v. 2) may either be an adjective (the cloud is "low with basalt and lava") or a substantive (the cloud is, figuratively, a "shoal" in color and form). Both "low" and "shoal" (or "reef") would cancel out the second (suggested) meaning. What the choice of "Base" does is 1. to suggest the "lowness" of the cloud; 2. to represent the solid "base" that is the form of the shoal; and 3. to, further, suggest the "baseness" of the (possible) disaster that has just (?) transpired, both from the *moral* and *sonant* (the "base" note that the trump [never] played) points of view. "Basalt" and "lava" are inverted, for the consonant-rhyme with v. 4. I have used "trump" (not "trumpet" or "horn") in v. 4 to suggest the two possible meanings of the French "trompe": the "high point" ("trump"), which corresponds, in context, to the "Suprême une," the mast, of v. 7; and the "trump(et)" (not) signalling the disaster. "Note" was selected (for "vertu") for the same reason: it preserves the two suggested meanings—1. the (musical) note of the "virtueless" instrument, and 2. the absence of "note" or "fame" (importance). Even the inconspicuous "y" (v. 6) may be ambiguous, meaning either "at it" (the foam—all that remains—is the only one who may know what happened, drooling "at" whatever transpired) or "there" (i.e., in the vast expanse of water that is the object of the poet's cosmic contemplation). My "thereat" conjoins the two in a single expression: it may mean either "at that (account)" or "at that place" (there). Further, "thereat," by its very form, suggests both "there" and "at (it)." It also contributes—for lack of a full rhyme—both assonant- and consonant-rhyme with "mast" (v. 8). "One supreme," not "Supreme (Highest) one," in v. 7: the latter, "correct" syntax, with adjective ("Supreme") modifying pronoun ("one"), fails to reflect the dislocation of the two in the French, which isolates the solitary pronoun. I have used "residue" (for "flotsam" or "wreckage"), in the same verse, for the rhyme with v. 5. "Abolit" (v. 8) may be either present tense or *passé simple*: the former is unlikely, though, not only because the wreck (which one?) has, we assume, already taken place (or not...), but also because it would not be consistent with the other *passé simple*, "cela," in the following verse. (This possibility will be discussed presently.) Also in v. 8, "dévêtu" means "stripped": literally, "unclothed." I have chosen the more literal latter word because "unclothed" contains within it the "cloth" of the stripped sail (cf. the "toile" of "Salut"), suggesting also the canvas, or paper, of the poet, which is, after all, at the "bottom" of all this (cf. the same verb, in the form of "vêt," in the final verse of *"Le vierge, le vivace et le bel aujourd'hui..."*). "Cela que" (v. 9) is curious and problematic (for reader and translator), as "cela" may function as pronoun or verb. It may suggest either 1. *"or* [else] *that* [other, second possibility: the drowning of the siren's flank] *which* [consists of the abyss' probable, or possible, drowning of the siren] or 2. *"or* [the shipwreck also] *hid* [the fact] *that* [the abyss will have drowned...]." "Hid that" both denotes the second possibility and, by an embedded pun, suggests the phrase, "Is it that." (The *that* may here be either the French "que" or "cela.") If "cela" is only seen as a pronoun (a mistake, I believe, eliminating all ambiguity, which Mallarmé surely desired here), the awkward "that that" may result, or perhaps "that which," which, unfortunately, may be confused with the French "ce que." "Lofty loss" (v. 10), for "high perdition," retains the alliterative effect "lost" when the "ƒuribond ƒaute" of v. 9 becomes English. As in so many Mallarmé texts, this poem ends in silence, with the (possible) drowning of the synecdochical flank of the mythical siren. A further suggestion of silence resides in the poet's use of the word "enfant." First, the usage is surprising in that the expression, usually a *substantive*, appears here as an *adjective* modifying "flanc." A rendering of "young" for "enfant" would eliminate this desired grammatical ambiguity. More important, the choice of the *child*-siren may well have less to do with her adolescence than with the etymological value of the word itself (the expression may thus be seen as a subtle reflection of the now-familiar entire *poetic* drama reflected by the ostensibly "cosmic" disaster): the source of "enfant" is the Latin "infans," meaning "silent" or "not speaking." The silencing (drowning) of the siren thus brings the reader in a full cycle back to the poem's opening verse with its equally curious participle of silence, "tu." And on what better "note" (or absence of one) to end a discussion of Mallarmé and begin one of Valéry than this one? For not only is Valéry also fascinated with this type of verbal ambiguity and suggestion, but he chose the very same word, with its etymological intimation of silence, in the celebrated opening verse of "Les Pas," to be discussed below.

PAUL VALÉRY

NAISSANCE DE VÉNUS

During the early stages of Valéry's writing career (i.e., the final decade of the nineteenth century), the poet produced a number of "exercises" later collected (in 1920) in the *Album de vers anciens*. In these poems, Valéry was not so much concerned with the themes of his later, more mature poetry (in *Charmes*, for example)—the mental processes, poetic inspiration, maturation, etc. Rather, he seems to have been preoccupied, in many of these texts, with the sensuality of sounds, with the effects of sound patterns of words and verses; in short, he was developing his own powers of "incantation." The four poems I have selected from this collection (the first four that appear in this volume) all reflect this quality and represent similar problems of translation. Moreover, these poems seem to have no "sens profond," no epistemological or metaphysical "pretext," no symbolic significance or metaphorical esthetic counterpart. They describe, or more properly evoke, atmospheres of sensuality, natural and feminine beauty, qualities of purity and splendor—all of which reappear in his later verse. "Naissance de Vénus" evokes the splendor and sensuality of the maritime birth of Venus, just as Rimbaud's "Vénus Anadyomène" parodically undermines feminine beauty by its ruthless description of Venus in the form of a tattooed tart emerging not from a seashell, but from a bathtub. Valéry's Venus seems to be given form—emerging from the storm that has spewed her out into the sun—by the very words and sounds chosen for her "portrait." First her skin, then her smile take form, followed by arms, shoulder, and hair. The tercets continue the evocation of her sensuous innocence, describing her leaping on the sand and her gazing at the sea, the womb whence she emerged.

The overriding problem of translating this relatively uncomplicated poem is the preservation of its wonderfully rich and evocative sonorities. (The poet in English who first comes to mind in this regard is Valéry's immediate predecessor, Gerard Manley Hopkins.) Still, in the very first verse, we are confronted with the ambiguous "mère," which simultaneously (and homonymically) suggests both "mother" ("mère") and Venus' actual mother, "sea" ("mer"). One way of rendering this simultaneous homonymy (or of approaching it, since it is impossible to realize in English) is to use "m(w)ater," or "mater"/

"water" ("mother-sea"). But this is too diagrammatic: my final choice of "sea-womb" brings to light the word play, although it does make it explicit. (I have, however, used the synecdochical "womb" for the more explicit "mother.") But it further produces an echo with "sea" (v. 3), which reflects the "mère"/"mer" echo in the same verses of the original. Sounds determine my word choice in the second verse: in the place of the sonority of the *t*'s (and the [ɛ]'s of vv. 2-3), I have produced the sounds emanating from the combination "fl*esh*... thr*esh*old... t*e*mpests... *b*eat/*B*itterly." Considerations of sonority likewise dominate the second stanza. Whereas *s* (vv. 5, 8), *b* (5), *p* (6-7), and *f* (8) echo in Valéry's stanza, mine bears the sounds of *s* (5-8), *b* (6-7), *o* (6), *t* (7-8), [ɛ] (7-8), *p* (7), and *r* and *l* (8). These patterns have, at times, determined the choice of words: the *cheville* "so" (v. 5); "slope" (for "rise," v. 6); "bewails" ("bruised"... "bewails"... "bewetted": Valéry's "éplore," a rare use of a verb that generally appears as past participle, is employed for its sonorous associations in the sequence "*éplore*"... "*or*ient"... "*é*paule"); "bewetted" (it is, as is Valéry's "humide Thétis," a redundancy inserted for the sound: to his *i* and dentals correspond my short *e*, *t*, and short *i*); and, finally, "precious jewels" (for "pierreries": the sequence "*p*ure"... "*p*reci-ous"... "tr*ess*" replaces the sonorous pattern of which the original French expression is a part). The same substitution of sonorities is effected in the opening tercet: a vocal reading of the stanza, in both French and English, should sufficiently demonstrate the point.

AU BOIS DORMANT

This poem presents another plastic evocation of mythical female beauty, this time of "sleeping beauty." Again, there is no "hidden meaning" here, no reflection of the drama of poetic creation or the mental process that we shall see in the later poems of *Charmes*. Valéry is preoccupied here with evoking sense from sound, with painting a picture of delicacy and hush in a background of natural beauty. The mysterious slumber of the princess is far removed from the hushed noises about her: as she composes the mysterious "word of coral," she is oblivious to the muted sounds and delicate movements that appropriately surround her—rambling roses (present in the opening stanza, they reappear in the final one), whispers and shadows, birds, splashing water, breeze, sound of flute and horn diffused by the gentle wind, descending sunlight. This is a picture of calm, mystical ("obscure," "Secrètement") repose, of regal ("princesse," "palais," "bagues d'or," "trésor") yet sensuous ("délice de plis," "sensible") beauty.

The preservation of sonorous effects is again the translator's chief problem in this sonnet. The opening two verses have sounds (alliteration, consonance) as their focal points; but whereas v. 1 presents no difficulties (since the sounds are the same in the equivalent English words), the second verse represents a conflict in the differing sounds of the two languages. The "murmurs" of the forest and the shades are evoked by a series of *m* sounds—"*m*ur*m*ures"... "*m*obile"... "o*m*bre"—that cannot be reproduced in English. I have rendered "murmures" as "whispers" and, consequently, produced a corresponding series of *s* sounds: "whi*s*per*s*"... "*sh*adow*s*"... "i*s s*leeping." The onomatopoetic effects are quite similar. ("Is sleeping" is chosen over the other present-tense form, "sleeps," both for the rhyme and the extra *s* sound it offers to the verse.) In v. 3, the adjective "obscure" is transformed into an adverb in my version, without semantic loss, for the rhyme with "roses" and for the rhythm of the verse. (Its present form is superior to the more literal "And an obscure word....") To preserve the assonance of v. 5 ("*éc*ou*te*"... "*g*ou*ttes*"... "*ch*u*tes*"), I have selected "catches" (closer to the French verb *happer*: cf. Corbière's "Rapsodie du sourd") over the more literal "listens to" in order to establish a series of assonantal *a*'s: "c*a*tches"... "spl*a*sh"... "c*a*scades." (The latter word was similarly chosen over "drips," "drops," and "chutes.") Alliteration produced by *f* and *v* sounds in Valéry's seventh verse—sounds that correspond, not by their specificity, but by their very echoes, to the wind and flutes' strains—becomes assonance (and "distant" alliteration, of *w*'s) in the English version; "diff*u*sed"... "fl*u*tes"... "l*oo*ming"... "w*oo*ds." Similarly, *r* becomes *m*, in v. 8: "*m*ur*m*ur"... "*m*ournful"... "*m*easure." ("Measure," rhyming with "treasure," was selected over "phrase," "strain," "tune," "tone," and "song.") Here, "mournful," not in the French text, is an admitted *cheville*. I have used it, however, in order to add another *m* to the verse. (There are already five *r*'s in the French.) Further, the French "cor," probably a "cor de chasse" or hunting horn, cannot be intimated by the simple "horn"; "mournful," then, additionally specifies the sound, which is here an obtrusive, undesired one. (We may compare, in a different, more somber context, the same horn's sound in Jules Laforgue's "L'Hiver qui vient," announcing the death of both the hunted stag and the dying autumn.) Finally, this possibility is confirmed by the "diane" of v. 9, which, besides denoting reveille, suggests Diana, "la chasseresse" (thus, the justifiable hunting context). Alliteration and consonance of *l*'s in v. 9 is preserved by the choice of the words "lull" and "reveille"; the appositive "long" (modifying "la diane") is purposely displaced in my version, as it is in Valéry's poem.

Some who have been tempted by the rhyme "sleeper"/"creeper" (for "liane") have misread "diane" as a reference to the princess herself; it is, rather, the sound that might awaken her and thus spoil this scene of regal repose. The rhyme (with this "correct" reading) is salvaged by "liana"/"lay on it" (v. 14). "Ensevelis" (v. 11)—"buried," as if in mortal slumber—is rendered as "shrouded heavily": the adverb is perhaps a bit "heavy," even rhetorical, but it does produce the only possible rhyme in English for "reveille." (The rhyme scheme had to be altered to this end.) "Plodding" was the choice for "lente," for the rhythm of the second half of v. 12. "Délice" becomes "treasure" (v. 13): a trochee is needed here; the princess's royalty is suggested; and my choice echoes the "bagues" of v. 4 and the "trésors" of v. 6. In v. 14, "sensible" is rendered as "yielding" (both expressions suggest a sensuous receptiveness), to produce the assonance (along with "r*a*ys"... "l*a*y") that corresponds to Valéry's three alliterative *s*'s.

VALVINS

Valéry wrote this poem in honor of his Master: it was solicited (along with 22 other poems) by Albert Mockel in 1897 for an album of verse dedicated to Mallarmé. Although there is a certain sensuality of description and (in the final stanza) an accent on sound patterns, the poem as a whole is atypical of Valéry's developing stylistic concerns seen in other pieces in the *Album*, simply because the poem was, it seems clear, intended primarily as a literary pastiche of its dedicatee. The title refers to the summer retreat of the elder poet, a tiny village near Fontainebleau, where Mallarmé spent many hours sailing on his small boat, the "yole" of the third verse. The poem is a testimony to both Mallarmé's life and poetry. The biographical allusions include the "yole," the "après-midi chanté" (referring to the afternoon "sung" by the Faun in Mallarmé's "L'Après-midi d'un faune"), the "voile" (both the "yole"'s sail and the white paper that so obsessed the poet: cf., for instance, "Salut"), the "brut azur" (a parallel poetic obsession), "silence," and the "livre" (yet a third obsession). Regarding the verse (and this is why I have referred to the poem as a pastiche), Valéry has been careful to insert, here and there, some of Mallarmé's favorite expressions and appears elsewhere to be trying to copy the Master's style. Examples include the playful, ingenious rhymes of the first quatrain, the displaced adjectives ("Heureuse," "Emue") in the parallel vv. 2 and 6, the familiar transitional "Mais" at the start of the initial tercet, and individual expressions both precious ("Selon que," "parmi") and purposely vague ("quelques," "quelque," "aucun").

The principal problem in the translation of "Valvins" is precisely the preservation of these Mallarméan touches. In the opening stanza, the problem is purely one of Valéry's imitative rhymes, which are playful and seemingly contrived or far-fetched. To retain this element—and it is important to note that it is such an essential and conscious aspect of the poem that other considerations of the translation such as semantic and sonal accuracy may be sacrificed with relative impunity—I have produced the equally (perhaps more) playful rhymes, "lets you aerate"/"literary" and "if y'are"/"afar" (to correspond with "qui t'aère"/"littéraire" and "si tu es"/"situés"). "Aerates you" had to be expanded to the less accurate "lets you aerate," for the more outrageous rhyme (although the sense of the verse is by no means distorted beyond recognition). Similarly, after playing (abortively) with "situated" for awhile as a rhyme in English, and after rejecting the rhyme "y'all (/Are)"/"yawl" (primarily because Valvins is much too far East of Texas!), I have settled with "if y'are"/"afar." Again, it is the ingenuity of the rhyme that is essential here, although "from afar" is a *cheville* of sorts and "y'are" a contraction not present in the original. Valéry's rhymes are, as are mine, more "for the eye than for the ear." In v. 6, the past participle "chanté" is rendered as a gerund phrase, "singing of" (afternoon): as Valéry wished to suggest, this version implies both the actual singing *in* the "faune" poem (by both Faun and poet) and the singing praises to (celebrating) the poem itself. "According as" is the seemingly stilted (but precious) equivalent of "Selon que" (v. 7), as "Amid" (v. 14) is the purposely awkward preposition that corresponds to the surprising but now-familiar "Parmi" that Valéry knew to be part of Mallarmé's poetic lexicon. In v. 11, the two adjectives "quelque" and "aucun," meant to suggest a typically Mallarméan vagueness, could both be rendered as "any" (i.e., it is not the *specific* work that is the focus here, but the problem of *écriture*, of writing any poem, on any sheet of white paper). To avoid this repetition, and to underline the strangeness of the negative "aucun" used as a "positive" (albeit "vague") adjective (cf. "Rien" of the opening verse of "Salut"), I have used "some" for "quelque" and "any" for "aucun." In the final tercet, "languorous" (for "long") adds the needed syllable for the verse's rhythmic consistency. (It also suggests the laziness of this summer setting.) More important, the *r*'s, *v*'s, and *p*'s of the Valéry text are replaced in mine by the alliterations of vv. 13 ("*s*ilty *s*kin") and 14 ("*l*anguorous *l*ook").

ETÉ

Although it would be a mistake to consider Valéry's poetic career as a purely linear development from one "style" to another, this poem of summer is, in a sense, a sort of "transitional" piece in that it incorporates the elements of plasticity and word sounds present in many of the poems of the *Album* with some of the expressions and more abstract considerations (ruminations) that surface in the later *Charmes*, and in particular the monumental "Le Cimetière marin." Regarding the latter, "Eté" is one of the first texts to ponder such elements as mass, movement, spatiality, and temporality (while retaining the sensuality of sound and subject already witnessed in the *Album* pieces discussed above). We also notice expressions that will reappear later in Valéry's verse: "pur," "ardent," "Espace," "tranquille," "crève," "rumeur." The ostensible subject of the poem (suggested in v. 3, but dominant in the final two quatrains) is a brilliantly sensuous young woman. But unlike the other poems of feminine beauty we have considered ("Naissance de Vénus," "Au bois dormant"), the "real" subject is not the woman herself, but the atmosphere that bathes her and the movement and activity informing this summer scene. It is a poem of sea and air (also a major part of the focus of "Le Cimetière marin"), and the dominant stylistic feature, besides the pattern of sounds, is a constant series of metaphors in which the poet transforms the summer ambience into a world of concretized entities: summer is a rock of air; the sea is first a hive of flies, then a mill of living organisms; the female flesh is a jug or urn; Space is a burning house; odors are circles; the day becomes huts; and air is a vine.

The buzzing of the first stanza is reflected by the buzzing of sounds: *r* (v. 1), *m* (v. 2), *c, ch* (v. 3), *b* (v. 4). I have thus predicated my choice of certain words ("*sw*eet" for "pure," to be heard before the "*sw*arm," for "hive," at the end of the first verse; "*S*cattered," to go with "*s*ea"; "*fl*esh *fr*esh"; and "*u*rn" and "*u*p," whose sounds lead up to the "*bu*zzes" of v. 4) on this essential aspect of evocation. For the (off-)rhyme, "urn" was chosen over the more accurate "jug" or "pitcher" ("cruche"). There may be a slight play on "mouches" (with "touffes"), which can also mean "tufts"; but this cannot be done in English. At any rate, the primary sense is "flies" (cf. the "ruche" of v. 1); and the "flies on" offers a convenient rhyme with "horizon." The reverberating *m*'s in vv. 7-8 are particularly noteworthy. Consequently, I have selected "*m*ur*m*ur" over "hum" or "din" ("rumeur") and "*m*ain" over "sea." The water's mass is again transformed in v. 8, from the flies of the first stanza to "herds": the latter term, with its insistence on bulk, was chosen over other possibilities ("troops," "throng," "flock") for the rhyme with "birds." "Tuns" (not "Casks") suggests, by homonymy, "tons": the same ambiguity is inherent in the French "Tonnes." Because I have had to place "pure nests" at the conclusion of v. 10 (for the rhyme with "rest"), I could not retain the parallel construction of the French ("qui mange et qui monte"), which would create a plethora of rhythmic beats in the verse. I have instead used an adjective ("hungry") and a gerund ("climbing") in the place of the relative clauses. As compensation, "h*u*ngry" (for "ravenous" or the like) echoes the sounds of "g*u*lf" and "s*u*n." The order of the breast and shoulders of the young woman in v. 14 is reversed, to place "shoulderblades" (for the rhyme) at the end of the verse. Nothing is lost, as the impression (as in a similar description of the two nymphs in Mallarmé's "L'Après-midi d'un faune") is one of fluidity and anatomical overlapping. "Of foam" (for "foamy"), v. 15, is chosen for the same reason. The evocative sounds of vv. 18-19 are partially preserved by the choice of "sti*tches*" for "links" ("mailles"), continuing the sounds of "ca*ges*"; and "*m*arit*ime*" for "marine" or "sea" ("marins"), both announcing "*m*ills" and echoing "br*ine*"... "B*y*." The final problem of translating "Eté" is presented by the rhymes for vv. 18 and 20: as there was no apparent solution for rhyming the basic elements "sea" and "air," I have used the synecdochical "brine" (used as well for its assonance and consonance, just discussed) and "air on its vine," which substitutes adjectival clause for adjective.

L'ABEILLE

A literal reading of this sparse octosyllabic sonnet reveals that its subject is a woman's desire to be stung by a bee. This is, to be sure, the entire "plot." But a closer reading tells the reader that the poem is not about a bee-sting alone. Nor about masochism, nor entomology. There is too much else implied (as is the case of many of the *Charmes*, which includes "L'Abeille" and the three poems that follow here: "Les Pas," "La Dormeuse," "Les Grenades"), including the very significant (for Valéry) elements—the *real* subjects of the poem—of awakening consciousness and the poetic process itself. Besides, it is indeed strange for the protagonist (first-person) of this poem written by a man to be a woman...

The major problem for the translator of this sonnet is to retain the ambiguity of many of the words, including those that describe the process of thinking and expression: "fine," "pointe," "sens," "alerte." The tmesis of the first quatrain ("What...ever") must be preserved, as it places special emphasis on the two adjectives "fine" and "mortelle": the sting—sharp *and* full of "finesse"—would both end the torment (the woman's and the poet's) of stasis and kill the bee itself. (Valéry believed that [like the bee] inspiration, and the poem in which it results, are short-lived, "dying" to give way to yet other thoughts and poems.) "Pointe" (v. 2) may mean both a stinger and an ironic *verbal* allusion; thus, the ambiguous "barb," which, as a bonus, brings the total of *b* sounds in the second verse to five. This is essential, for it preserves the richness of sounds of the original "soit *t*a poin*t*e, *b*londe a*b*eille." "Corbeille" (v. 3) poses a difficult problem: it may mean "basket" or "flowers" or "balcony." And it means *all* of them, in the context of the poem: describing the woman's sting-thirsty breast (cf. v. 5), "corbeille" suggests a container of plenty, the succulent object of the bee's search, and the female "balcony" (whence the French colloquialism, "il y a du monde au balcon," "there's a crowd in the balcony," said of a woman with large breasts). Because there is no English word to express all this, I have settled for the figurative "balcony," which shares the aspect of cantilevering with the breast and presents no problem of interpretation for the reader. To compensate for the loss of the other connotations, I have translated "tendre" not as "tender," but as "delicate," which may bring to mind that quality of the *flower* that attracts the bee to it. In v. 5, "gourde," a metaphor for the roundness of the breast, may mean "gourd" or, in its nineteenth-century usage, "flask." The latter was chosen primarily for the off-rhyme it makes with "flesh" of v. 8. I suspect that the rhyme is the reason for the inversion of v. 5, so I have not retained this syntax in my version; cf., however, the more dramatic use of inversion—retained in translation—of v. 8 of Mallarmé's *"Le vierge, le vivace et le bel aujourd'hui..."* "Offense," "misery," and "agony" parallel the nearly-synonymous French "offense," "mal," and "supplice" and were chosen for the rhyme. "Sorely" (not "really") adds a slightly inappropriate pun, not present in the French; but it is far less prosaic than the other options and does contribute to the woman's anticipation of a *physical* awakening of her consciousness and sensuality by the bee's sting. In v. 12, "illumined" and "sense," although they look like slavishly literal translations, were selected to preserve the double meanings Valéry intended: the first term may connote both elucidation (of consciousness) and the light radiating from the *golden* bee's sting; while "sense" may be, as in the French, either sensorial or cerebral. The same simultaneous consideration of these seemingly conflicting drives is present throughout Valéry's verse (cf. "Les Grenades," to follow). The penultimate verse presents us with the final problem of the poem. "Alerte" may mean "alarm" or a "situation of danger." It connotes both apprehension by the receiver and aggression by the donor. A situation of martial antagonism is implied; and, as a periphrasis for the sting itself, "raid" captures this ambiguity, as well as providing an off-rhyme with "fades."

Les Pas

Like "L'Abeille" and "Les Grenades" (and many of Valéry's poems, notably "Aurore" and "Palme"), "Les Pas" is a poem about anticipation and preparation—in particular, like the other poems, the creative preparation of the poetic mind. The poet must be patient, must allow his thoughts to mature slowly before putting them into words. Analogous to the mix of inspiration and labor is the coexistence of sensual and cerebral experience, which is, here again, an integral part of the text. Ostensibly a poem about a man who awaits his lady (the changes of personal pronoun from start to finish, and the entire fifth verse, suggest that what the poet awaits is a being loftier than a mere female—perhaps inspiration itself?), there are hints that it is not a love poem (despite the sensual and tender elements throughout), but rather a poem about silence and expression, awaiting and receiving, preparation and anticipated consummation, patience and desire. In fact, the "human" protagonists fade in the face of the more important subject of the *process*, perhaps the major preoccupation of Valéry the poet and the thinker.

As the "ombre" of v. 5 suggests, it is the "shades" of meaning, so delicate and elusive, that present the major problems of reading and translating—as well as the beauty of—Valéry's poetry. This text, like many of the others in *Charmes*, is composed (literally) of delicate networks of sounds and subtle shades of meaning, combining to express the human—and poetic—drama of *becoming*. The first verse presents the reader with a typical problem. The footsteps, which the poet awaits at the outset (and, indeed, even as the poem ends), are described metaphorically as "enfants." Literally "children," this expression not only denotes this phenomenon (the poet's silence has "given birth to" the concept of anticipation), but it also connotes silence (soon corroborated three words later), a major theme in the poem, from its Latin etymon, "infans," meaning "not speaking." (The same usage occurs often in Mallarmé's poems, notably in the final verse of *"À la nue accablante tu..."*) "Infants of my silence" is one possibility, although here the emphasis would be on the diminutive status of the child rather than on the metaphorical significance of the expression (i.e., that the products of the poet's silence are precisely the footsteps of the "intruder"). What my "stillborns" (clinical as it may at first appear) does is to maintain the theme of birth and pensive production; to preserve the theme of silence ("still"); and to imply that even at the moment of "conception," the *thought* is just that—unspoken, unexpressed, at this point without a life of its own. (And, indeed, these "children" are not living, but metaphorical.) "Mute" (v. 4) was chosen to avoid repetition with the "silent" and "still" of v. 1. What of "Personne" (v. 5)? Literally, it presents no problem; but the word in French is a versatile one and is used as such by a poet of Valéry's subtlety. It may mean "person," or "no one," or "anyone": Valéry does not mean here a "real person" (it is followed by the appositive, "ombre *divine*" [my emphasis]), but rather a being, a presence, even a feeling. The more viable solution, then, is not "person," but "one," which both suggests a vague, indeterminate being, even an absence (of specific identity); and substitutes a repetition of identical terminal letters ("o*ne*...divi*ne*") for the original alliteration ("*P*ersonne *p*ure"). Regarding "Presage" (v. 7), "await" and "anticipate" are also likely contenders for the assonant-rhyme with "shade." But "presage" (for the French "devine," to guess or foretell or divine) not only retains this meaning, but it is also a verb that specifically represents the process of mental perception that is, after all, the central focus of the poem. "Proffered" (v. 9) expresses the *potential* energy of the kiss, as it may mean both "offered" and "essayed." Another process—that of intellection—is rendered by the two English words "dweller" ("habitant") and the gerund "thinking" ("pensées"), not "thoughts": both expressions carry over the concept of thought as a *living*, developing process. (We should note the evolution, from the silence and stasis of the initial verse.) The "de" of v. 15 is a curious substitute for the expected "pour" ("in order to"). It is not the *purpose* of the poet's life to await the tender being; it is, rather, his life that has derived its meaning *from* the single source—inspiration?—of the anticipation itself. (Valéry uses the word "patience" elsewhere, implying a kind of patient suffering or endurance, from the Latin verb *patior*.) And what can be made of the unexpected switch in personal pronouns, in vv. 15-16? The various pronominal and verbal forms of the familiar second person ("tes," "tu," "hâte") that precede now become the formal "vous" and "vos" of the final two verses. This sudden formality, indicating that the awaited being is not simply a woman, but, ultimately, an object of veneration and respect—perhaps an abstraction— necessitates the change to "thee" and "thy," the only alternatives to the English "you." These terms, in English, imply a vaguely religious, even a literary experience—appropriate to the text—and the "thee" also supplies a convenient rhyme with "be." A final note on a fair exchange: the effort to preserve these niceties of meaning and connotation is not without sacrifice, as I was not able to retain the *very* "rich" rhymes (in French, "millionnaires") with which Valéry has endowed this lovely poem.

LA DORMEUSE

Again consistent with the thrust of many of the poems in *Charmes*, "La Dormeuse" is concerned not only with the apparent subject—another "sleeping beauty"—but primarily with the dynamics and conflicts of the phenomenon of slumber itself (cf. "Neige," to follow): sleep/wakefulness; body/soul; absence/presence; and, in particular, the dynamics of potentiality, as mystery, silence, inactivity, and dream all conceal the "real" woman and suggest the drama of possible "becoming," of an anticipated transformation into the complementary conditions of certainty, speech, action, and awaking into the world of reality. The poet/persona seems to be a kind of third party: it is not he who "watches over" the female presence (or absence), but the corporeality of the woman that watches over the "dreaming self." The poet's function is, rather, one of questioning (the form of the opening stanza) and of expressing and evoking the phenomenon of sleep that occupies his mind... and pen.

"Aspirant" (v. 2) is an interesting choice made by Valéry and presents an equally interesting choice to be made by the translator: I have retained the English cognate, as I believe that Valéry must have wished to make his word an ambiguous one, suggesting both the breathing in or sniffing of the flower (in the woman's dream) and the "aspiration" to equal the flower's beauty by her somnolent presence. (Francis Ponge uses the same term to similar ends in "L'Orange," to describe the orange's ambition and squeezing processes.) The rhyming in English of the opening stanza also presents problems. The *rimes embrassées* of the original quatrains have thus been converted to *rimes croisées*. I have translated "chaleur" not as "warmth," but as the semantically not-too-distant "bloom" (for the rhyme with "consume," chosen over "burn"); and have chosen "woman in slumber" over "sleeping woman" ("femme endormie"), for the consonant-rhyme with "flower." The evocative sounds of vv. 5-6 must be preserved: for Valéry's *s*, *i*, *t*, and *p* sounds, I have substituted the following echoes: "Brea*th*"... "vi*s*ions"... "hu*sh*"; "*vis*ions"... "*inv*in*c*ible"... "tranquillity"; "h*ush*"... "*l*u*ll*"; "*tr*iumph"... "*tr*anquillity"... "*te*rrible"... "*te*ar." As this preservation is absolutely essential in the light of the sonorities of the original text, (slight) sacrifices in semantic accuracy had to be made in the following word choices: "visions" for "dreams" ("songes"); "tranquillity" for "peace" ("paix"); and "terrible" for "powerful" ("puissante"). The ninth verse is even more extraordinary for its sonorities. Valéry must have liked it very much, as he gives us a rather similar verse in another of the *Charmes* (which, after all, suggests, from its Latin etymology, "songs"), "La Fausse morte" (v. 3): "Que d'ombres, d'abandons, et d'amour prodiguée." Corresponding to Valéry's four *d*'s, three *r*'s, three *m*'s, and two *b*'s are my five *s*'s (three *sh*'s, one *sl*, and one *st*), three *r*'s, two *i*'s, and two *t*'s: "Slumberer, shimmering store of shadows and shifts." To create these reverberations, I chose "Slumberer" over "Sleeper," "store" over "heap," "shimmering" over "golden," and "shifts" (the movements in sleep to which the female body abandons itself) over "abandons." I believe that there may well be a play on the word "biche" (v. 11): its primary meaning is, of course, "doe" or "hind" (the metaphor here refers to the nervous, perhaps delicate "abandons" of the sleeping woman); but it may also be employed as a term of endearment or affection ("ma biche": cf. "mon petit chou"). *My* "dear" denotes the latter term of affection and suggests its homonym, "deer," which corresponds to the primary meaning (although not in the ideal feminine form) of "biche."

Les Grenades

The process of thought—its development and maturation—is the fundamental subject of this sonnet by Valéry. Its form—often criticized for its "repetition"—is significant: the central image is expressed in typically poetic terms in the first quatrain, in which the poet compares the bursting of the pomegranates to the bursting of "sovereign brows" (the heads of poets) and, consequently, the products of the fruits' maturation (seeds) to those of the minds ("découvertes," or thoughts). Then, for the remainder of the poem, the process of development and bursting is analyzed in some detail (Valéry is, quite literally, an "analytical" poet, as is Proust in much the same way in prose), with the final tercet returning to the original statement of the simile. This structure underlines the concept of *process* (vv. 5-12), framed by the similar statement of poetic analogy at the start and finish of the poem. What should interest us here, and what will be the focus of the discussion of translation, are the problems of poetic language, in the end the great concern of all great poets. Ambiguity, word play, effects of sonority, and shades of meaning will again prove to be of vital importance, for Valéry and for his readers.

The poem's first word represents a rather subtle problem: "Dures" means—literally—"hard," but by an intended homophony it may also suggest duration (that essential aspect of maturation, from the French verb *durer*). "Hard" will not preserve this polyvalency (the hardness of the pomegranates' covering and the duration and patience of the ripening process), but "Firm" will, as it may mean, from its two basic definitions, "hard" as well as "fixed" or "unchanging." The second word (and title) of the poem is also more problematic than it might at first appear to be. "Grenades," in French, can mean "pomegranates" (the primary meaning, in the poem's context) or "grenades." The secondary meaning seems to me to be an essential lexical strategy on the part of the poet, as the themes of bursting, conflict, struggle, endurance, and violence—inherent in the process of maturation and birth—are so central to the poem's language ("Cédant à l'excès," "E-clatés," "subis," "travaillées," "Craquer," "force," "Crève," "rupture"). I have thus taken the liberty of creating a neologism—"pomegre*nades*"—which is a rare device for Valéry, but which nonetheless here succeeds in combining the desired dual meanings of fruit and bursting grenades in a manner superior to that of other possible (and rejected) alternatives. "Uncoverings" (for "découvertes," v. 4) deserves some explanation. Valéry often uses prefixes to affirm both the literal and figurative meanings of words that begin with them. Here, "découvertes" means, figuratively, "discoveries" (i.e., the thoughts of the poets); and also, if we separate the prefix from the rest of the word, literally, "dis-coveredness," or the action of being "uncovered," the skin bursting and revealing the seeds. The literal translation, "discoveries," carries across the first meaning, but not the second. "Uncoverings," on the other hand, succeeds in retaining both meanings: "uncovering" may be a synonym of "discovery" in English; and it may also, as gerund, denote the physical rupture of the cover, or the rind, of the fruit (and, similarly, the opening of the mind, revealing the products of cogitation). The disjunction of vv. 7-8 is intentional ("Have made you *with pride inured* / Crack..." [my emphasis]), as it is in the French. "Inured" was chosen not only for the *rime riche*, but also for the implication of a "difficult or painful" experience, which is precisely what the fruits endure through their patient and proud ripening process beneath the sun. Moreover, the word's etymological source is, felicitously, the old French *ovre*, or "œuvre," "work" (cf. "travaillées"). If the second quatrain emphasizes the agent of the maturation and bursting (the sun), the first tercet focuses on the bursting itself. We should note in passing that Valéry is not speaking merely of fruits; the "sovereign brows" of poets are always part of the analogy, hinted at by "sovereign" words like "pride," "ruby," "gold," "gems," and "luminous." (We recall the "illuminé" of v. 12 of "L'Abeille.") Nowhere in Valéry's poetry are sonorous effects more significant or more sensual than in the first tercet of "Les Grenades." If I have failed to retain the alliteration of vv. 5 ("Si les *s*oleils... *s*ubis") and 8 ("*C*raquer les *c*loisons..."), I have tried to compensate for this by preserving the rich series of internal sound repetitions (assonance and consonance) of vv. 9 and 11. The first problem of the ninth verse is the enigmatic use of "que." Because the initial tercet is a continuation of the conditional clause of the second quatrain (the sentence skeleton should read "Si..., et si..., cette... rupture...," "If..., and if..., this... rupture..."), and because the "que" is not preceded by any expression *including* it that may then be truncated as "que" (e.g., "lors*que*... et *que*," "when... and when"), it must be that there is no semantic or grammatical reason for "que"'s being there at all. This pleonastic "que" does have a *poetic* reason, however: it adds to the verse one more [k] sound, emphasizing the hardness of the outer covering of the fruit. Untranslatable as far as meaning goes, "que" becomes, in my version, a second "and," which (without adding any "meaning" to the verse) produces a similar effect: it contributes an additional ("hard") *d*. (Although the English verse now stammers slightly, the presence of the second "and" as a word with no contributable meaning, used merely for its sonority, represents a certain faithfulness to the original text.) "Dried," not "dry," was selected for two reasons: first, for the extra *d* sound; second, whereas "dry" is merely a descriptive adjective, "dried" suggests a passivity and "patience" as well as the presence of an implied agent (the sun), phenomena already introduced by the "endured" of the fifth verse. I have chosen "rind," not "skin" or "bark" or "peel," for the same reason: here, the *ri* sound echoes that of the preceding "d*ri*ed," and the terminal *d* continues the echo just mentioned. Comparing the English and French verses, we may conclude that although the letter *c* might be more effective than *d* in mimetically reproducing the illusion of "dryness," nevertheless the evocative echoing of internal sounds is approximated in the translation: the French has a repetition of two *s*'s, two [k] sounds, and two *or* sounds; while the English repeats *d* three times, *nd* three times, and *ri* twice. As for the eleventh verse, the sensuous [ʃ] sounds of "gemmes" and "jus" have easily been approximated in their English cognates ("gems," "juice"). But "rouges" is a bit of a problem: "red" does nothing for the English verse's sound pattern. (Here, the translator must place sound over meaning in his choice, as long as the proper, or at least approximate, shade of red is preserved.) Roget's *Thesaurus* gives no fewer than forty-five different shades of this color; from them, I have selected, I believe, a happy solution to the problem—"magenta." A purplish-red not far from the hue of the fruit in question, it not only retains the sensuous *j* sound *and* the *m* and *e*, all three of which are echoed in the very next word ("gems"); but it also suggests "majestic," which is, after all, totally suited to the entity analogous to the fruits (the "sovereign brows" of v. 3). The French verse, then, contains four sound repetitions (as does the English): two *r*'s, two *e*'s, three *j* sounds, and a near-assonance ([u]/[y]); while my version includes three *j* sounds, four *s*'s, two *m*'s, and two *e*'s. As for the difficult thirteenth verse, "âme" does not denote here the literal "soul" we find as the primary dictionary meaning. I am not entirely certain of what Valéry had in mind, but the word "mind" does come to mind. The precise meaning of "âme," in context, is elusive, so that an approximation must be the fate of the translated version. But it is clear that the context strongly suggests the aspect of cerebration and the thinking *process*. (After all, Valéry's own mind is one of these "sovereign brows.") The "compromise" of the word "mind" is, I think, adequate, especially since it offers a convenient rhyme with "rind." The surprising use of the past definite tense—"j'eus"—indicates that thoughts are made to be matured, to burst from the mind, and to dissipate, to be things of the past, giving way to new ones continually. (This is an essential feature of Valéry's theorizing about the thought process.) The term, in fact, reflects the cyclical structure of the poem itself. I suspect that Valéry also had the rhyme (with "jus") in mind here. My "former" expresses this life/death or present/past process, while at the same time allowing "mind" to remain as an end-rhyme.

LA CARESSE

The final two poems I have translated in this volume are from neither *Album de vers anciens* nor *Charmes*: they appear in two collections casually put together by the poet, consisting of poems and fragments written at various points of his literary career—*Pièces diverses de toute époque* ("La Caresse") and *Mélanges* ("Neige"). The first text, "La Caresse," is the sole anomaly in this volume of translations in that it requires relatively little commentary. I have chosen to include it here for two reasons: it is a lovely little poem, to be read for its sonorous qualities and its delicate expression; and it is my surrogate choice for the too-long (for this format) "Palme," with which it shares the fundamental theme of the palm tree's solace and swaying majesty. This slight poem has neither the grandeur of "Palme" nor the latter's philosophizing about the phenomenon of maturation, so dear to Valéry the thinker and poet. But it does recall, in even more intimate and sensuous terms, the admiration of the poet for the tree in "Palme" and is particularly reminiscent of the second stanza of the latter poem.

"La Caresse" is among the shortest of Valéry's poems in terms of syllable count: it is written in heptasyllables, and my version (for the only time in this volume) is rendered, for the most part, in corre-sponding dimetrical verses. The only stanza that merits a commentary is the final one. The palm's caress has the effect of attenuating "le mal" into simple melancholy. This soothing function of the palm is incorporated into the rhyme, with the *cheville* "soothed" rhyming with the "smoothed" of v. 10. ("Smoothed" is, likewise, chosen over the more obvious "polished.") The most obvious feature of the stanza, however, is the sonorous quality of vv. 9-10. I have selected "dread" over "evil" for the assonance/consonance of "dread"/"spreads"; this is appropriate not only because the expression in the original draft of the French poem was not "le mal" but the less strong "la douleur," but also because the change in the French was *also* made, surely, for reasons of sonority, "Et le m*al* s'é*tale, tant*" being more evocative than "La douleur s'é*tale tant*." Similarly, "As" ("Comme") replaces "Like" for the additional *s* sound, just as "*s*lab" ("dalle") is chosen over "flag" or "stone" (and, again, "*s*moothed" over "polished"). The resulting series of sounds is quite close to its French counterpart: the five *a* sounds of the French correspond to the five *s* sounds of the English; and where the sounds of "*é*tale" and "t*ant*" (v. 9) may be (and indeed are) compressed into "*é*tend" of the penultimate verse, so the "*s*prea*d*s" and "su*c*h" of v. 9 of the English version conjoin to produce the "*s*tre*tch*" of v. 13.

NEIGE

"Neige" is the only poem presented here that is written in *rimes plates*: I have preserved this important element throughout, with true rhymes in vv. 1-2, 5-6, and 13-14; off-rhymes in vv. 3-4 and 9-10; and consonant-rhymes in vv. 7-8 and 11-12. The essential feature con-veyed in this lovely sonnet is movement—a controlled transition from one thought or psychological state to another. The real "subject" of the poem is not, as the title would have us believe, a simple action: something *has* happened—snow has fallen overnight. Rather, like many of the better-known poems of *Charmes* such as "Les Grenades" and "Palme," "Neige" is really a sequence of thoughts, one giving way to another, about an ostensibly simple phenomenon. The bursting of the fruit and the subsequent projection of its seeds, the maturation

and subsequent descent of the tree's fruit, and the descent and subsequent accumulation of the snow are all stimuli to Valéry's analytical
mind and awakening consciousness and are characteristic subject matter for his poetry. A conscious control of form, structure, and sonorous effects permits Valéry to modulate from the expression of an
exclamatory inner thought triggered by the spade's noise that awakens him, v. 1 (a comment on the morning silence), to the description
of his awakening consciousness, vv. 2-5 (the awareness of the snow
outside), to the mental reconstruction of, and wonderment at, what
must have transpired overnight, vv. 6-11 (the arrival of the snow that
now covers the ground), to the attempt at reconstructing the life
inside the houses that the snow has covered, vv. 12-14 (the poet's view
of the snow and what it is hiding). The result is a desired (and typical)
hesitation between thought and action, exclamation and description,
looking out and looking in, cold and warmth, and harshness and
innocence: these elements of antithesis and transition (already witnessed in some of the poems of *Charmes*) are unmistakably characteristic
of Valéry's poetic expression.

The opening verse awakens the poet, not only with the sound of the
spade, but also with the *s*'s and *b*'s, which in my version are *s*'s and *o*'s.
The essential word in the verse is "battu": Valéry has chosen this
expression rather than, say, "rompu" or "percé," for its ending—
"tu"—which echoes, so to speak, the silence, now shattered by the
spade, which opens the poem. (Silence becomes the major motif of the
poem: cf. "sans bruit," "sourdement," "sans voix.") My choice of
"trans*muted*" denotes the *change* from silence to noise and affords the
verse the same echo ("silence," "muted") that appears in the original.
"Simple" is rendered as "sole," since Valéry is using the word, as he
often does (cf. "candeur," v. 10), in its etymological sense, here from
the Latin "simplex," or "single." (I have chosen "sole" over "single" for
the *o* sound.) The additional rhythmic and sonorous echoes in Valéry's opening two verses ("bat*tu*"/"atten*du*," "n*eige* fr*aîche*") are present in my series "transmu*ted*"... "a*wake*"... "a*waited*" and in the consonance of "*new snow*." Likewise, in the next two verses, the contrast-
ing sounds of the poet's somnolent warmth ("*chère cha*leur") and the
snow's harshness ("*d'une du*re") are reflected in my "*w*ondrous
*w*armth" and "bleakne*ss* har*sh*." "Durent" (v. 7) was chosen with consummate care by Valéry. Its primary meaning in context is as the *passé
simple* of the verb *devoir*, denoting the number of flakes the skies
"must have lost" overnight. The word has two additional connotations, however: it suggests both the long period of time (from the verb

durer) during the night in which the snow has seemed to fall (consistent with the motif of expansive time are the rhetorical "combien de flocons," the inclusion of the adjective "toute," and the hyperbolic expression describing the snow, "pur désert," in apposition with "flocons"); and the cold hardness (from the adjective "dur") that has disturbed the poet's "chaleur" and that echoes the "dure" of v. 4. My separated verb form "Must... have endured" is comprised of, in the first part, the verb of probability (cf. *devoir*) and, in the second, the element of duration. (The secondary meaning of the English "endure" is "last," "continue," "remain.") The third connotation, that of hardness, is lost (although the primary meaning of "endure" is "to bear" or "to undergo," which suggests a "hard" ["dur"] experience); it is, however, belatedly recuperated in the final verse ("Hardly"). "Blo*t* ou*t*" is chosen for "wipe" or "erase" (v. 9) in order to add a *t* series to the sequence "enchan*t*ed"... "*t*race," thus preserving the repetition of the same letter in Valéry's verse ("*t*raits"... "*t*erre"... "enchan*t*ée"). "Candor" (v. 10) is retained, since Valéry is using it in its etymological (Latin) sense of "whiteness." The sonority of "sourde*ment* aug*men*tée" is reflected in my choice of "*se*cretly incr*eas*ed": this consideration took preference over the fact that "secretly," although suggesting the anonymity of the nocturnal phenomenon (as does "sourdement"), does not carry over (at least *explicitly*) the element of "absence of sound." "Awoke" is not precisely what is suggested by "accoutumée"; but it does imply the poet's mental reconstruction of a "dormant" family life in the houses (covered by snow) whose chimneys are the only hint of habitation and activity, while allowing for the rhyme with "smoke" (v. 14). In the final verse, "A peine" may be translated as "barely," "scarcely," or "hardly." I have chosen the latter because it more precisely reflects the original intent of the poet: to echo the "*Dur*ent" of v. 7 by the use of the expression "A peine," an adverb in which the substantive ("peine") suggests the *hard*ship or the general motif of the snow's aggressivity and harshness, which contrasts with that of (the poet's) warmth and coziness now so suddenly disturbed by both the snow and his own awakening consciousness.

SELECTED BIBLIOGRAPHY

PRIMARY SOURCES

Charles Cros, Tristan Corbière:Œuvres complètes. Ed. Louis Forestier and Pierre-Olivier Walzer. Bibliothèque de la Pléiade. Paris: Gallimard, 1970.
Stéphane Mallarmé:Œuvres complètes. Ed. Henri Mondor and G. Jean-Aubry. Bibliothèque de la Pléiade. Paris: Gallimard, 1945.
Paul Valéry:Œuvres I. Ed. Jean Hytier. Bibliothèque de la Pléiade. Paris: Gallimard, 1957.

SECONDARY SOURCES

The purpose of this section is not to offer references to detailed exegeses. It is, rather, to help the general or scholarly reader fill the gaps purposely left by the format of the present undertaking, i.e., with introductory discussion concerning biographical data, summaries of the various poems that are more detailed than the brief résumés I have given before each analysis, historical or literary-historical information, and the like, that may be consulted for "background material." Titles concerning Corbière are indeed (too) scarce; the volumes dealing with Mallarmé and Valéry I have selected are, I believe, the most helpful among the mass of others written about these two ever-popular poets.

Tristan Corbière

Macfarlane, Keith H. *Tristan Corbière dans "Les Amours jaunes"*. Paris: Minard, 1974.
Mitchell, Robert L. *Tristan Corbière*. Boston: Twayne, 1979.
Rousselot, Jean. *Tristan Corbière*. Paris: Poètes d'aujourd'hui, Seghers, 1951.
Sonnenfeld, Albert. *L'Œuvre poétique de Tristan Corbière*. Paris: Presses Universitaires de France/Princeton University Press, 1960.

Stéphane Mallarmé

Cohn, Robert Greer. *Toward the Poems of Mallarmé*. Berkeley: University of California Press, 1965.
Fowlie, Wallace. *Mallarmé*. Chicago: University of Chicago Press, 1953.

Michaud, Guy. *Mallarmé*. Paris: Connaissance des Lettres, Hatier, 1953.

Mondor, Henri. *Vie de Mallarmé*. Paris: Gallimard, 1942.

Noulet, Emilie. *L'Œuvre poétique de Stéphane Mallarmé*. 1940; rpt. Brussels: Jacques Antoine, 1974.

Walzer, Pierre-Olivier. *Mallarmé*. Paris: Poètes d'aujourd'hui, Seghers, 1963.

Paul Valéry

Berne-Joffroy, André. *Valéry*. Paris: Bibliothèque Idéale, Gallimard, 1960.

Charpier, Jacques. *Paul Valéry*. Paris: Poètes d'aujourd'hui, Seghers, 1956.

Grubbs, Henry A. *Paul Valéry*. New York: Twayne, 1968.

Lawler, James R. *Lecture de Paul Valéry, une étude de "Charmes"*. Paris: Presses Universitaires de France, 1963.

Sewell, Elizabeth. *Paul Valéry*. Cambridge: Bowes & Bowes, 1952.

Whiting, Charles G. *Paul Valéry*. London: The Athlone Press, 1978.